DOORWAYS TO SIN!

By
Samantha V. Evans, Ed.D.

COPYRIGHT

Names, characters, businesses, and places are used in a fictitious manner with the exception of the names Dr. David Allen and The Family Group who have given permission. No part of this book may be reproduced, or stored in a retrieval system, or transmitted in any form or by any means, electronic, mechanical, photocopying, recording or otherwise, without the express written permission of the publisher. Bible quotes used in this book are from the King James version.

Text Copyright © 2018 by Samantha V. Evans, Ed.D.

ISBN 978-1725968509

All rights reserved.

Published by Samantha V. Evans, Ed.D.

Cover design by AGP Bahamas (Affordable Graphics & Printing)

The first edition

DEDICATION

A story of how a generational curse impacts your life, and the road to forgiveness and deliverance through Christ, Jesus.

This book is dedicated to every human-being who suffers under the afflictions of generational curses but are now committed to learning how to break those evil covenants with Satan and shut those doors so that they can receive forgiveness and complete deliverance.

TABLE OF CONTENTS

Dedication..3
Acknowledgements...7
Foreword..9
Introduction...11

SECTION 1:
Naivety – Brainwashed and Manipulated!

Chapter 1: College Life in Atlanta.......................................15
Chapter 2: Meeting Dwayne the Charmer.........................18
Chapter 3: Battered at Bruised at Twenty-One................22
Chapter 4: What a Tangled Web we Weave…!................28
Chapter 5: She Big-up, Big-up!..35

SECTION 2:
Reclaiming My Power: God Favored Me!

Chapter 6: If You Fail to Plan..42
Chapter 7: Breaking Free...47
Chapter 8: No More Scales on My Eyes............................60
Chapter 9: Break Out!...65

SECTION 3:
Spiritual Awakening – Sold Out for Christ!

Chapter 10: Self-discovery and Healing............................69

Chapter 11: Battling to Save Souls for Christ................................73

Chapter 12: Fake it Until You Make it!....................................78

SECTION 4:
Vulnerability – Getting Weary in Well Doing!

Chapter 13: Tears of Joy..82

Chapter 14: Satan Initiates his Plan to Destroy Me.......................87

Chapter 15: Getting Married..97

Chapter 16: Satan Came Home with Me.....................................102

SECTION 5:
Matters of the Heart – Broken and Shattered!

Chapter 17: Stabbed in the Back by Family...............................115

Chapter 18: Recovering from Surgery While Under Attack..................122

Chapter 19: Reality Check...129

Chapter 20: Sealing the Deal..134

Chapter 21: To Date or Not to Date......................................140

SECTION 6:
The Original Doorway!

Chapter 22: Please Don't Touch Me There.................................145

Chapter 23: Elementary School Days-Acting Out and Becoming
  a Bully...152

Chapter 24: Pre-teen Years – My First Taste of Love.....................155

Chapter 25: Withdrawn and Depressed.....................................158

Chapter 26: Teen Years – Rebellion of the Black Sheep................162

Chapter 27: Senior Year – My First True Love..............................166

SECTION 7:
Complete Deliverance: The Final Fight for My Freedom Through the Blood of Jesus Christ!

Chapter 28: The Jezebel Spirit..170

Chapter 29: Discovering and Breaking the Generational Curse..174

Chapter 30: Tormented and Intimidated by Evil................179

Chapter 31: Quiet Reflection – God Never Left Me...............192

Additional Doorways to Sin..197

Biography of the Author..210

Acknowledgements

Writing this book was a heart wrenching journey through my past and a form of therapy at the same time. As reluctant as I was to write this book, writing it made me realize that I had not yet fully healed from past hurts and that I was still battling strongholds in my life. I recall praying over the years, asking God for divine connections. I knew that was important but had no idea that those divine connections would be connected to my deliverance. Hence, I want to thank a few of those persons who played a pivotal role in helping me to get on and stay on the path to winning the most important battle of my life.

Firstly, I must thank my sister from another mother; Mrs. Esther Wheeler. This mighty woman of God was sent into my life to fulfill her own purpose as a writer then God used her position in my life to help me to discover some very important pitfalls in my life. Her being in my life has been such a blessing, that there are no words to explain the many things God has revealed to me through this divine woman.

Secondly, I must acknowledge my dear friend and colleague Sonia Storr. What can I say about this mighty woman of God other than we were meant to band together to fight in such a time as this. She was my strength when I was weak and encouraged me to write my book and stay on the fiery line when I didn't feel like going on or when recalling past hurts became too painful. Your words of encouragement were sent straight from heaven.

Thirdly, to my pastor Rev. Dr. Vaughn Cash and my church covering at Evangelistic Temple. Since I moved back to Nassau and began attending this church, I have grown tremendously in Christ. When you enter this edifice, you know that the Holy Spirit dwells there. Additionally, it is important to be shepherded by a true man of God and there is no doubt that we get that at my church. Sir, I pray that you will continue to let the Lord lead you as you shepherd the flock.

Finally, to my three children-my angels who God entrusted me with. There aren't enough words to express how much I love you all. The many battles I have fought in my life, the evil covenants I have broken, and the many strongholds I have cast down have all been to secure your future. I refuse to allow any of you to have to fight ancestral battles like I did. It was out of ignorance, in many instances, and others selfishness, that such evil covenants were made so I chose to fight for us. I refused to be selfish. From this point on, we will live our lives based on the laws, principles and promises of the Most High God so that our lives will be blessed!

Foreword

George Eliot – "Don't judge a book by its cover."

Sometimes in life we look at people around us and do the exact opposite of the above quote from George Eliot. Whether it's the colleague in the cubicle next to us, a fellow student in a classroom, the neighbor next door, or just someone we meet for the first time, we have the human tendency to draw conclusions based only on what we see.

People may look great or terrible on the outside but on the inside, there could be a whole lot of life experiences that have affected or shaped that person's life's journey which will give us a different picture of who they are if we only knew. The mistake we often make is that we simply size people up without ever hearing their life story up to that point. This is the mistake that the Prophet Samuel made in 1 Samuel 16 when the eldest son of Jesse was presented to him as a possible future King of Israel. However, God's response was, "The LORD does not look at the things man looks at. Man looks at the outward appearance, but the LORD looks at the heart." The point is that there is so much more to a person's life than what we see on the outside.

Dr. Samantha Evans in "Doorways to Sin" has very courageously and transparently unveiled her life's journey for her readers up to this point in her still relatively young life. In this book you will read about her personal experiences inclusive of the good and bad. She openly shares the bad or wrong choices and decisions she made over the years that resulted in lots of personal disappointment and pain. You will share in both her struggles and how she persevered through them, her wounds and her healing, her victories and her defeats, along with the powerful testimony of how God delivered her from the bondages that held her captive and set her free to embark upon the next phase of her life characterized by this spiritual, mental, emotional and physical freedom.

Dr. Evans also uncovers for her readers how some of her experiences might be exactly what they might be going through right now in their lives and how they can also be delivered and freed. She exposes the traps of Satan and how people are sometimes snared therein without even realizing that they're being seduced or enticed. She also explains how things happen at different points in life which are forced upon us by authority figures who might be loved and respected which can lead us into bondages even though we were not directly responsible for what happened to us or what we might have been led into.

What I see in this book is a clear manifestation of the grace and mercy of God extended to Dr. Evans in very tangible ways as he ministered his love, patience, forgiveness and healing culminating in her decision to totally surrender her life to him after years of vacillating and inconsistency in her relationship with him. The good news is that God is willing and able to do for you exactly what he has done for her and set you free to live for and serve him with all your heart, soul, mind and strength.

Congratulations Dr. Evans and my prayer is that God will use your story to positively impact the lives of thousands of women like yourself (and men) so that they too can experience the liberating power of Jesus Christ.

Rev. Dr. Vaughn L. Cash
Senior Pastor Evangelistic Temple
Nassau, Bahamas

Introduction

The Lord said in Jeremiah 29:11: "I know the plans I have for you; plans to prosper you and not to harm you. Plans to give you hope and a future." I always knew that God had a great call on my life but for some reason I had to fight hard for everything I achieved. I really didn't understand it. I just thought it was normal. I walked through my young life very mischievous, withdrawn and afraid but as a teenager I became a Christian. I was committed to my walk with God yet I felt a burden on me that I couldn't explain. I felt fearful and that I was never alone, but I couldn't explain it. However, I loved the Lord and had a huge desire to serve Him.

As I got older and started college, God started to show me flashes of my past through my dreams. Every year, during the same month, I had a recurring dream. Years later, the Lord fully restored my memory and I remembered that I was sexually abused as a child. At that moment, so many things about my life became clear but it would take decades for me to learn that that one incident was a doorway through which sexual sin entered my life. This first doorway served as the initial entry point and that first access point became a passage way or portal for other such kindred spirits to enter my life. Hence, I wouldn't only need salvation, I would also need deliverance!

As more spirits were given access into my life through my actions, Satan then had dominion in my life. As more and more spirits entered my life, a fortress was erected and a principality then ruled in my life. This principality is the strong evil spirit that became the ruler over the other evil spirits that were given access through doorways over the years. The main ones that operated in my life were anger, rejection, hurt, pity, arrogance and pride, and oh, let's not forget FEAR!

However, evil spirits could be any vile ones you allow to enter into your life such as an adulterous (cheating) spirit, a homosexual spirit, a lying spirit, a suicidal or defeatist spirit, a spirit of manipulation, a lazy spirit, a spirit of low self-esteem, a drinking spirit, or a spirit of violence. Hence, it is important to know the Word of God and how to utilize God's promises to protect yourself from such horrid spirits.

My brothers and sisters in Christ, when God told me to write this book, I was afraid to but He reminded me that He didn't give me a fearful spirit and that many persons are depending on this Word that He gave me for their deliverance so I chose to be obedient. I have learned over the years that obedience is better than sacrifice. Furthermore, I love God so much and it is my heart's desire to serve Him in spirit and in truth. It is my prayer that you will be blessed from reading this book and pull what is needed from it to strengthen your walk with God.

I do not profess to be an expert in anyway on the things of God or the spirit world, however, I am an expert on what I experienced in my life and a true living testimony of how God delivered me from being destroyed by strong evil forces that were determined to kill me. My journey to this point of complete deliverance was not an easy one but I can tell you that once you commit yourself to Christ and allow Him to deliver you, teach you and strengthen you daily, remain in His Word and in fellowship with other believers in Christ, pray without ceasing, and continue to praise Him especially when you feel like giving in or turning back, you will be able to stand up to Satan, fight those demons off and eventually they will flee from you.

SECTION 1
Naivety: Brainwashed and Manipulated!

Chapter 1: "College Life in Atlanta!"

I can't remember exactly how old I was when it happened. All I can remember is that I was young; no more than eight years old. My first memory of anything traumatic happening began as a dream while in college in Atlanta, Georgia. I dreamt that I was in this small wooden house with only four rooms. The exterior of the house was sea green and the rooms were very small. The front portion of the house was well lit with natural light coming in through the screen door and two single windows, but the back of the house, where the kitchen and a small bedroom were located, was dark and scary.

In the dream, I would walk through the house to the dark bedroom and slowly push the door open. There is an old man lying on the bed, motioning me with his hand to come towards him. As I begin to walk towards him, the next thing I know is that I am falling from a high place, but before I hit the ground; I wake up frightened and confused. I had that dream once every year for twenty-four years. I didn't understand what it meant at the time so I dismissed it.

At nineteen years old, I was starting my junior year of college and excited to be in Atlanta; the ATL! However, I had the culture shock of my life when I arrived because I had never lived away from home before so experiencing the African-American culture first hand was intense. I am from Nassau, Bahamas; born and raised. I grew up with both of my parents in a sheltered environment so I really didn't have much street knowledge. You could say that I was a bit naïve but I can tell you that I had a great deal of wisdom.

I enjoyed college life in this city, even though many of the students were wild and loose with their educational opportunities. I could not understand how students could come to college and behave so crazy! I mean they drank and partied all the time. I couldn't even imagine wasting time, money or my education in such a frivolous way; my parents would kill me! My housemates were no better. I stayed in a rooming house. My roommate was a Bahamian so we got along fine but the rest of them didn't really seem too concerned about learning. There were people in our house all the time to the point that it was scary coming out of my room sometimes just to use the bathroom.

It was a quaint stone house with about five bedrooms, two bathrooms and a kitchen. It had a front porch which was great to sit under to watch the sunset or to enjoy the evening breeze, but really who had time for that when I was always taking a ridiculously full load of classes up to eighteen credits to be exact! I was a smart student so making a 4.0 GPA was a no brainer. My first year was wonderful! My roommate and I stayed to ourselves and focused solely on our classes. We hung out on the weekends and joined a club started by Bahamians living in that city. This was a great way for us to connect with other Bahamians at our school and in the city. We had a lot of fun as a group.

It was now my senior year and I had developed an interest in singing professionally so I took part in an audition at my college but was so nervous and scared that I failed miserably! I was upset with myself because I knew I did badly and needed help. I started looking in the newspaper for vocal lessons so that I could develop my skills. That was when I met HIM; the man who would change my life drastically.

Chapter 2: "Meeting Dwayne the Charmer!"

I remember calling the number from the newspaper to inquire about vocal lessons. The man on the end of the line had a deep, soothing, professional voice which made me feel very comfortable. I told him that I was interested in singing and needed some help. He asked me if I had ever recorded before and I told him yes very briefly but I didn't like the work that was done.

Some months earlier, I had had a few sessions with a man who lived nearby. Honestly, I can't even recall how we met. He, along with the sessions, was so unmemorable that I can only write one sentence about it. Hence, that led me to look for a better (and hopefully) more skilled producer.

I made an appointment to meet with the man who I will call Dwayne who did not work nearby. In fact, I had to get on a train and several buses to get to his studio, but I was determined to get the assistance I needed. The meeting went well and we arranged to begin my sessions. The first few months of sessions were great! I loved the progress we were making. However, something else was happening.

I found myself becoming quite fascinated by Dwayne's skills to the point that I was intensely attracted to him. Now at this point we had already engaged in much conversation so he knew about me and I knew about him. He was in his forties at the time and I was twenty. He had three children and was going through a divorce. Based on the information he shared, he stated that he had "an itch that his wife could not scratch." Even though I was young, I knew what that meant; he was not sexually fulfilled. Well, I don't know what I was thinking but I got this crazy notion that I could scratch that itch for him so from that point on, I changed the way I dressed from conservative and safe to slightly sexy and enticing. I used subtle charm to see if he was interested in getting to know me better and it worked!

It didn't take long after that for things to heat up between us. I didn't even know I had this hot pepper in me to entice anyone but here she was in living color. I had no idea where she came from but she was me. Hence, I looked forward to my recording sessions with great anticipation and as feelings of lust surfaced, it wasn't long before Dwayne and I were engaged in activities of a carnal, ungodly nature. I knew it was wrong but I did it anyway. The connection between us quickly mushroomed into a full-fledged relationship. He was now my man!

Need-less-to-say, I was excited because he made me feel like the queen I knew I was. He catered to my every need and from that point on, I didn't have a transportation problem because everywhere I needed or wanted to go; he took me. Dwayne and I grew inseparable and at this time, I even forgot that he had children or had to be discreet due to his pending divorce.

Subsequently, I started making demands of him which seemed to pose a challenge for him. All I wanted was more of his time outside of studio time which he had difficulty doing because he started getting calls from his wife to come home to cater to the needs of their three children.

"Now wait a minute," I thought to myself.

Something wasn't right about this situation. My antennas began to rise as I wondered what was going on. When I asked him about it, he told me that he had to comply until their divorce became final. I accepted his answer with no reservation.

A few months afterwards, I graduated with my Bachelor's Degree. Once the ceremony was over, I went home to Nassau for a short trip to visit my parents and to look for a job. In a matter of days, I got a call from Dwayne telling me that he missed me and wanted me to return to Atlanta. Shortly thereafter, I returned to Atlanta to spend what I thought would be some quality time with him.

I still had my room at the rooming house but my roommate was preparing to move out soon so I told Dwayne that I could stay there or look for another place to stay. Well, since he wanted me around him all the time, he decided to move me into his studio while we looked for an apartment. I was excited but little did I know that this man was setting me up for years of hurt, loneliness, regret, and physical and sexual abuse in a way that I could not even begin to imagine.

Chapter 3: "Battered and Bruised at Twenty-one!"

I spent what seemed to be every waking hour with Dwayne. He was so charming, smooth, and sexy. Anything I wanted I got. Wow, this is the life I dreamed of! Well, so I thought. I remember the first time Dwayne put his hands on me. It was a sunny summer day in Atlanta, Georgia. I can't recall, what we were doing but we were in his car just cruising around. We stopped at a gas station to get some snacks. We both went inside. When we returned to the car, he opened the door for me then went around to his side to get in. Once in the car, I felt a hard arm across my chest.

Wham! I gasped for air as that blow almost took the life out of me. Dwayne had drawn his arm with as much force as he could and struck me in the chest. I was too afraid and short of breath to ask what happened. However, when I did, he said that I embarrassed him.

"What?" I thought to myself, "he has to be insane!"

From that day, on my life changed and Dwayne became a man of a different demeanor and temperament. I no longer knew who he was or how to act around him. It seemed that everything I did from that point on was wrong and angered him. Should I be afraid for my life? That was a question I could not answer as yet.

Dwayne did not always act this way. There were days when he would bring me flowers and chocolate, buy me anything I wanted, take me out to eat, and spend candlelight romantic nights with me, but there were times when he would leave me alone without food for days. I can remember one holiday the first year I was with him. It was Thanksgiving Day I believe. I had a little job at the Chinese Restaurant that had just opened next door to his studio but they were not open that day so I had no food. I called him repeatedly that day, but he refused to answer his phone. He left me alone that entire day without any food to eat.

He showed up the next day like nothing had happened. I asked him what happened yesterday and he told me as clear as day that he had to spend that day with his family. That was the day I realized that maybe I was not as important to him as he had stated. Maybe this relationship was just one of convenience for him. I started to slowly get depressed. Well, after he dropped that bomb on me, he tried to smooth it over by taking me out to eat and spending the day with me but the damage had been done.

From that day on, I started to reconnect with my ex-boyfriend who lived in Tampa. He was a great distraction amidst the foolishness I was now going through. Of course, Dwayne didn't see it that way. He again saw it as disrespect on my part. I was in my element, sitting on his work phone at night talking to Allen, when he left me alone!

About a month later, I got a job at McDonalds which wasn't my first choice but it was a job. Business at the studio had slowed down so Dwayne couldn't do those lavish things for me that he did initially. I needed a job. Even though I had my Bachelor's Degree in Psychology, it was difficult finding a job so I took the first thing that became available. I became a McDonald's employee which surprisingly I enjoyed. One of the best things I liked about it was the free food I got when I worked the late-night shift. That was awesome! A few months into the job, I was able to afford an apartment so I moved out of Dwayne's recording studio.

My apartment was lovely. It had two bedrooms, a living room, dining room, kitchen and a private backyard. I finally started to feel like I was making some headway in my young life. Dwayne was back to being a gentleman and life was good again. I started to realize that once I didn't ask him about the progress of our relationship; he was a happy camper. However, I was not raised to live in sin so I was now concerned about this hole I was sinking deeper into. In spite of my concerns, I continued to see Dwayne and allow him to feed me the stories he did about his divorce being delayed.

I can remember one evening while off from work, I decided to spend some time with him at the studio. He had some guest recording artists in from Alabama who were working on a single. The trio were all men. I sat there as they recorded and as the hour got later and later, I started to tire so I stretched as normal people do. At the time, I didn't see anything wrong with having a good stretch but a fury was boiling in Dwayne unbeknownst to me. As I continued to wait for him, I began to doze off then sometime later, I heard the door close which indicated to me that the group had left. I was so tired but happy to finally get to my bed.

I got up from the love seat and was met with Dwayne's hand in my face. He slapped me so hard that I almost fell to the floor but he grabbed me, shook me like a rag doll and placed me on a stool. I started to cry uncontrollably because firstly, that slap hurt and secondly, I had no idea why this man was hell bent on hurting me. That was the night Dwayne tortured me until daybreak because in his eyes, I had embarrassed him in front of clients.

As bewildered as I was, I could not fathom how I had possibly done that! This time I didn't have to ask. He willingly told me what I had done. He stated that when I stretched, that was a sign of disrespect where he is from. It was an indication that I was showing these men my breasts and enticing them. Now wait a doggone minute! As shocked and grief stricken as I was, I said to him,

"But I was only stretching! I was tired!"

Because I didn't see what I had done wrong, this man shook me so forcefully that I started to feel dizzy. In his fury, he took the opportunity to talk about the calls received from my ex-boyfriend Allen on his work phone and even accused me of sleeping with him. I was totally distraught but he didn't care. He continued to shake and hit me in the face to the point that my lip started to bleed.

He then told me that he heard me on the phone one night talking to Allen and it sounded like we were getting back together. He made it clear that that was not going to happen. At this point, he took a loaded gun out of a drawer and put it to my head and said angrily,

"I could kill you right now and no one would ever find your body."

At that moment, I accepted the fact that my life was over because this man was going to kill me. I could see the evil in his eyes. I was so weak and tired from him hitting me and from not sleeping that I really didn't care anymore. My eyes were swollen from crying and him hitting me, and my lips were swollen and bleeding as well so if this was the end then so be it.

I cried and cried and as I cried in agony suddenly, he took the gun from my head and removed the bullets. It was like he was in a trance and had caught himself. All he did from that moment was apologize and apologize some more. He then went outside and threw the bullets into the bushes next to the studio. I could not tell what time it was because the studio had no windows. When he came back inside, he went to the bathroom, and got me some tissue for my face. I don't know how long it took me to catch myself but when I did it was bright outside. This man had literally tortured me all night long!

I was exhausted but I couldn't sleep. I had a girlfriend driving in for a visit in a few hours. Dwayne knew this but didn't care. He was determined to teach me a lesson. After he took me to my apartment, I went to the bathroom to take a bath. When I saw my face, I began to cry some more because I looked like I was in a fight and lost. Since I wore glasses, I could hide my eyes but how was I going to hide a busted lip?

After I took a shower, I got ice from the freezer to put on my lips to help with the swelling. That worked but my bottom lip was still torn from him hitting me. A few hours later, Pharra and her boyfriend arrived and spent a few hours with me. She didn't know how to ask me about my bruised lip but eventually did. Of course, I didn't tell her the truth. I lied and told her that I had walked into a wall. I knew that lying was wrong but how could I tell anyone that I had just been beaten and tortured all night by the man I loved. I was so confused. I spent the next few days in bed sleeping and allowing my body to heal from that horrible experience.

Chapter 4: "What a Tangled Web We Weave…!"

I never experienced anything like that again with Dwayne but he had already planted the seed of the fear of him so deep within me that I was afraid all the time. I tried my best to not make him angry which was hard because I really didn't know what made him angry. He would still hit me but it wasn't as bad as being tortured. I did stop communication with Allen in Tampa but I still had communication with some of my family members. However, I never told them that I was being abused at Dwayne's hands. I learned to play the survival game to stay alive, keep him happy and my family in the dark.

I found myself feeling sad a lot and wondering if God had forgotten me. After the abuse escalated I started praying more and more. I don't think I prayed for God to get me out but to keep me safe. I also asked God a series of questions. Why is this man abusing me God? What is going on God? Where are you God? I remember one night having a dream that I was in the car with Dwayne and God showed me this white shield he had around me. In fact, the shield was around the whole car. That brought me some level of peace and comfort as it made me realize that amidst all of my pain and confusion that God was protecting me.

One day, I was at the recording studio having a good day hanging out with Dwayne, but noticed that he was irritated more than usual. I didn't know what was wrong. I was a bit concerned because we had not had any abuse issues in a few weeks which was good and I wanted to keep it that way. I did notice that he was snappy a lot more than usual so I tried to stay out of his way and comply as best I could with what he wanted.

Dwayne had specific sexual needs which I did my best to meet. He had a very high sex drive and expected me to do things that I was not experienced doing or felt comfortable doing in some instances. If I ever told him "no", he would force himself on me which was painful so I never told him no again. Since I was young and inexperienced (with only one relationship under my belt), I did not know how to perform oral sex which he loved. Consequently, he started the emotional abuse calling me stupid and incompetent, saying that I don't love him because if I loved him then I would want to please him and not leave him feeling unfulfilled.

These words were very damaging because I hated doing this for him but complied to keep the peace. However, every time I did it, I heard how inadequate and incompetent I was. I started to hate him and dreaded every time I knew he wanted to have any kind of sexual encounter with me. The only time sex was enjoyable was when there was no oral sex.

A few months later, I discovered that Dwayne had another bad habit. I grew up very sheltered but there were certain scents that I was familiar with and that was the smell of marijuana or "weed". I started to smell that scent around him a lot more but it was too faint to identify initially, but it was familiar. Anyway, I dismissed it. While at the studio one day, he stepped outside for a minute then he got a phone call. I opened the door to call him and lo and behold, this man was smoking a joint! This is the same man who had told me when we first met that he didn't drink or smoke. Oh, what a tangled web we weave when first we practice to deceive! This was the first of many lies to come.

After living in my apartment for about nine months, I moved out when I got another job closer to town. It was a job in my field where I managed a program for youth on state assistance. It paid well and I got to use my expertise. My life again started to show progress; well so I thought.

In less than six months, that job ended when the program lost its funding but shortly after that I got a job at Kinko's. At that time, Dwayne was paying my rent at a rooming house which was decent. He preferred paying rent by the week rather than monthly since they required less upfront fees. It didn't matter to me as long as I had a place to stay.

A few months later I lost that job. I was just having what seemed to be a lot of bad luck keeping jobs. I was now solely dependent on Dwayne for my survival which meant that he had to pay for my rental. This was posing a challenge for him and after missing two weeks of payment, I was asked to leave. I was becoming more depressed so I planned to go home for a while to look for a job and to think because I was sinking deeper into this hole and didn't know how to get out.

I left Atlanta in December 1995 and spent Christmas at home for the first time in a long time. When I arrived home, it wasn't long before I got a job selling medical and dental insurance with a new company. This wasn't what I wanted to do but I needed a job. I had also applied to graduate school in Atlanta so I was prayerful that I would be accepted.

I worked with the company for about four months before Dwayne called asking me to come back. At this point I was really tired of the insecurity regarding our relationship so I told him that he needed to take care of his divorce first then we could talk further. Again, he fed me a story that it was near completion so I didn't have to worry much longer. I believed him. Not only did I believe him but I realized that I was in love with him.

In spite of all the abuse, I had suffered at his hands, he treated me well otherwise. He was doing very well musically (for the most part) and I accompanied him to all of the promo events, clubs, recording sessions, beautiful homes in Atlanta and on out of town trips. That lifestyle was so nice. I loved it and wasn't ready to give that up!

With Dwayne constantly asking me to come back and the fact that I was unhappy with my job, I quit and returned to Atlanta. I can't remember where I stayed when I got back but at some point, I moved into his studio again. This time, his business was located in the area where I lived when we first met which I was familiar with.

This move to the inner city proved to be a bad one because that life style that I had gotten accustomed to had faded away over the four months I was gone. I don't know what had happened in my absence or why he moved to that area. I didn't ask and he never gave an explanation. All I knew was that life started to get extremely hard.

To add, I started to feel sick all the time and my clothes started to get tight especially across the mid-section. I couldn't figure out what was wrong. As long as I could remember, I was very petite; wearing a size -2 to zero. I was tall in stature-5'7" to be exact, brown skin, weighing about 110lbs. I was always athletic so I was slim-built. I wore my hair natural but it was braided mostly. Now my clothes were posing a challenge for the first time which was odd but I dismissed the feeling (as usual).

One Saturday afternoon in the spring, Dwayne was having a fun day at his recording studio to attract clients. He had free food and drinks with live music. It was supported by locals which was promising. However, as the day started to wind down, I saw this slim lady walking up the sidewalk towards the studio. She wore jeans with an African print top with her hair wrapped with the same print cloth and sandals. She had three children with her. For some reason, I felt like she was his soon to be ex-wife. I can't explain it; I just knew. When she got to the door, she asked for Dwayne. I asked who she was then she introduced herself as his wife – Vicky – and asked who I was. Me with my smart mouth said boastingly,

"I am his girlfriend and you won't be his wife fa much longer because y'all divorce almost final!"

She replied shockingly: "What divorce? No one is getting a divorce. We are happily married."

"Well shut the front door," I said to myself!

I looked at her bewildered. If the floor could have taken me under at that time I would have fallen straight to hell! I argued with this woman telling her that she was a liar and that Dwayne told me that he filed for divorce over a year ago and that he said that the papers would be finalized soon. To my surprise, Vicky told me all about her relationship with Dwayne, how many nights they have sex, their plans for the future and all she thought she knew about me.

Vicky knew about me because I answered the phone most times when he was not there. I recalled her calling and asking for him one day then questioned me a bit. I honestly can't remember exactly what I said to her but knowing me, I probably said something that I shouldn't have (like I am his girlfriend). At that point, I was ready to start my life with Dwayne so she had to go!

That day was already rough for me since I was feeling sick so her lies pissed me off even further. She called for Dwayne who appeared from the studio to find me and Vicky standing there and without any of us uttering a word, he knew that he was caught! He had been lying to both of us and had no way of getting himself out of this tangled web he had woven. The cat was now out of the bag!

Chapter 5: "She Big-up, Big-up!"

The next day I woke up with serious pain in my stomach and uncontrollable vomiting. If I didn't know any better, I would think I was…..!

"Nope! No-No! There is no way that could be the case," I thought to myself.

Dwayne did not sleep at the studio that night. I guess being confronted by me and his wife was too much for him. He spent the night at home. When he arrived the next morning, he met me in the bathroom vomiting. I told him my suspicion and he told me that I needed to go to Planned Parenthood.

"Lord, what was happening?" I asked myself.

I was having an emotional meltdown at the very thought of my thought and what it meant. I didn't want to jump to conclusions so I got dressed and went to the clinic. Once again, I couldn't get my pants to meet which further confirmed my suspicion.

When I got to the clinic, all of my suspicions came full circle. The nurse gave me a test that confirmed that I was pregnant. Not only was I pregnant; I was almost six months pregnant! The nurses in the clinic were all in panic mode as they couldn't believe that I didn't know that I was pregnant and had not received any prenatal care up to that point. I am sure they exactly what I said to her but knowing me, I probably said something that I shouldn't have (like I am his girlfriend). At that point, I was ready to start my life with Dwayne so she had to go!

That day was already rough for me since I was feeling sick so her lies pissed me off even further. She called for Dwayne who appeared from the studio to find me and Vicky standing there and without any of us uttering a word, he knew that he was caught! He had been lying to both of us and had no way of getting himself out of this tangled web he had woven. The cat was now out of the bag!

Chapter 5: "She Big-up, Big-up!"

The next day I woke up with serious pain in my stomach and uncontrollable vomiting. If I didn't know any better, I would think I was…..!

"Nope! No-No! There is no way that could be the case," I thought to myself.

Dwayne did not sleep at the studio that night. I guess being confronted by me and his wife was too much for him. He spent the night at home. When he arrived the next morning, he met me in the bathroom vomiting. I told him my suspicion and he told me that I needed to go to Planned Parenthood.

"Lord, what was happening?" I asked myself.

I was having an emotional meltdown at the very thought of my thought and what it meant. I didn't want to jump to conclusions so I got dressed and went to the clinic. Once again, I couldn't get my pants to meet which further confirmed my suspicion.

When I got to the clinic, all of my suspicions came full circle. The nurse gave me a test that confirmed that I was pregnant. Not only was I pregnant; I was almost six months pregnant! The nurses in the clinic were all in panic mode as they couldn't believe that I didn't know that I was pregnant and had not received any prenatal care up to that point. I am sure they were thinking the worse but their thoughts couldn't be as bad as mine because I didn't want to be pregnant for a married man. What was scarier was that I would have to break this news to my parents. At twenty-three years old, I had no job and I was pregnant in a strange land! To add, I had no idea what I was going to do.

The next four months of my pregnancy were surreal. All I remember is that I was having a baby. That became my focus. I had already missed nearly six months of critical care for my baby so I had to ensure that I did everything else right until delivery day. That meant me not getting into any fights with Dwayne. Even though I was angry with him for lying to me, he was not priority anymore.

At seven months, I went home to visit my parents for a week and when my dad saw me he was very angry. I can't remember him talking to me at all while there. My father had great dreams for his children so I knew that he was disappointed because he felt that I had ruined my life. I didn't like feeling like a disappointment so I had a task on my hands, and I knew that after I had my baby that I would have to prove him wrong.

When I returned to Atlanta, life became even harder and as each day went by, business steadily plummeted at Dwayne's studio. I moved into another rooming house as the studio was no longer an appropriate place for me to stay. There was no phone so I could not contact my family. Whenever I called them, I had to be sneaky about it so that Dwayne would not find out. He had convinced me that he was the only one who loved me and that my parents would try to pull us apart if I told them how I was living so I never did. I believed him. I remained in the rooming house for several months; but two-weeks shy of my due date I was evicted. At this point I was frustrated and lonely. I didn't know where I was going to move to because Dwayne had no money. This was a disaster!

I was so dismayed but I had to find somewhere to stay. I found out about a homeless shelter where I could stay. It was in a church and very safe. I had never stayed in a shelter before and couldn't understand how I arrived at this point of homelessness. I had no answers.

I believe that my faith in God was being challenged at this time. I admit that I had not been committed to my relationship with God so maybe He was trying to get my attention. Dwayne had managed to ostracize me from my family so I was in this alone. This time in my life was so dismal that I don't know how I survived other than by the grace, mercy, and favor of God.

I moved into the shelter without telling Dwayne. When I told him, he was furious but there was no alternative because he had no money and at that point he was openly seeing both me and his wife. Such blatant disrespect and disregard! I was feeling really hopeless so I started going to church.

I met a nice lady by the name of Janice. She became like a mother to me which I think I needed at the time because my decisions were not all good since Dwayne had me brainwashed. Dwayne didn't go to church and I don't think he liked the fact that I went. He was too busy smoking weed and trying to live a lifestyle that he could no longer afford or maintain. I had to face that reality and quickly realized that I needed out of this relationship.

While staying at the shelter, I started to have peace of mind and less stress. I had gotten accepted into graduate school so I spent most of the days in class and the others walking through the mall looking at maternity and baby clothes then went to the studio to see Dwayne before going back to the shelter in the evening. I was on scholarship so money was tight. When I got money sent to me by my parents or my older sister Brenda, I didn't tell him because I knew that if I did, he would use it to buy weed.

Instead, I used it to buy clothing for my baby and maternity clothing for myself. By keeping the money received from my family a secret, I was able to eat three meals a day and keep my baby well nourished. I gave God thanks every day for the support I got from my family even though I was very secretive about my relationship with Dwayne. I was embarrassed. How did I get here having an affair with a married man? God was going to charge me for sure!

On September 16th, 1996, I gave birth to my baby girl – Alice. She was beautiful! My water broke while getting ready for bed at the shelter. Once I told the shelter manager what had happened, an ambulance was called for me. The pain was only intense for a short while as I was quickly given an epidural once I arrived at the Grady Hospital. It was heavenly.

I gave birth to my baby girl by the 1-2-3 count of the lovely nurses on the maternity ward because I could feel nothing. I was showered with so much love over the week I stayed in the recovery section of the maternity ward and my daughter was given everything a baby could need and more. God had indeed shown us favor!

On the day I was discharged, Dwayne did not pick me up. He stated that he had nowhere for me to stay so I called Janice who came to get me and opened her doors for me and Alice to stay. I stayed with her for several weeks which was great as she showed me how to take care of my daughter in the absence of my mother.

Janice was a Godsent! I even got to call my parents, who I hadn't spoken to in a while, to tell them the good news. Furthermore, I got some much-needed sleep while with Janice especially since she took great care of my daughter. Life was great!

Unfortunately, it was short lived as Dwayne soon called stating that he had a place for me to stay. I was sad yet excited because Janice lived far away from my college which would have been a challenge getting to and from classes. Sad because I had to go back to Dwayne's world which had proven to be most stressful and abusive. Never-the-less, I went but the apartment that Dwayne prepared for me to move into with a new baby would have been rejected by the dead-it was hideous!

SECTION 2
Reclaiming My Power: God Favored Me!

Chapter 6: "If you Fail to Plan…"

You would think that the apartment that Dwayne had secured for me to move into with our daughter would have been a mini mansion but it was a dump! Let me find the right words to do this place justice. Oh, did I say it was a dump?! It was a tiny building on top of a store front. It had not been used by the owner for a long time so it was in bad shape. When I walked into the building there was a sofa there and it was decent. The room was narrow so with the sofa there you had to turn sideways to get into the back part of the unit.

Now here is where the scary started. The entire back part of the unit was gutted so all of the rotten wood was exposed. The bathroom was so small and horrible that I can't remember it enough to give a description. There was a twin bed in the small bedroom with a bassinet for Alice. There was a small window to the left of the bed overlooking the street. It was the cutest room in the place and the room where I spent all of my time.

What made my stay in this rat-infested unit bearable was that my mom and sister Brenda were coming to visit. I had gotten furniture donated from my church for the apartment and I was exempt from attending class that semester since I had just given birth to my daughter so I was elated! When Brenda and my mom arrived, they had to stay with me in that horrible unit. The one good thing that came out of their stay with me was that once they returned home, my parents and working siblings agreed to pool their resources together to get me a nice apartment. Dwayne was pissed because my family now despised him for having me live in such unkempt quarters.

As soon as I was fully healed and moving around well, I started looking for an apartment in the vicinity of my university. I found a beautiful two-bedroom apartment that was perfect for me and Alice. Once we moved in, life started to change drastically. I began to devise a plan to get away from Dwayne because he had no desire to change his life. It was clear that he was addicted to marijuana and I knew that if I stayed in that dead-end relationship that my future would not be a healthy one.

To not draw suspicion to myself, I became very compliant to his every need and desire. At this point, he knew that he was losing his hold on me so he started secretly following my every move especially when I went to classes at the university. He especially took note of the males I spoke to while on the university compound. He was beginning to become very possessive.

I remember having to take Alice to class with me on numerous occasions but thanks to my wonderful professors, they understood that I was a single mom raising an infant. Again, God showed me favor! On one of the few occasions when I didn't have

Alice with me to class, I found myself feeling free and normal again. I toyed around with the thought that I could really break free of Dwayne and have a real relationship with a stable guy.

I felt so normal that after class, I had a great conversation with a cute classmate in the parking lot. He was tall and slim with chocolate brown skin. He was a breath of fresh air. I was waiting for Dwayne to pick me up so he decided to wait with me. He was a teacher at a local school and unmarried. Interesting! Anyway, even though I was quite fond of him I knew that this was wishful thinking. Let's be for real, I had a child and a paranoid possessive man in my life who accused me of liking every man I saw or spoke with. I was miserable!

By the time Dwayne arrived, my handsome classmate had left but guess what? Dwayne had been sitting in the distance watching the entire exchange. I was accused of using classes as a way to meet men. Heaven forbid I was actually going there to learn something or to get my Master's Degree! Oh, no, that would be absurd!

For the rest of that evening, I was called every foul name imaginable from whore to slut to a liar. This became a normal thing for the duration of my college life and what made matters worse was when I bought a car. Thanks to Janice, I was able to purchase my first car.

I started working as a Graduate Assistant in my department in January 1997 as a result of a five-star recommendation given by my graduate advisor. To add, I was also recommended for a fellowship which I was granted. God showed me favor yet again. Each time God showed up in my life, it gave me more strength to know that I could get out of this dark hole I had been sinking in for three years.

I had gotten so good at pretending that I started to lose touch with reality in a way. Over the next two years, I etched a plan to disconnect from Dwayne and break free. He had no idea what I was doing because like I said, I had gotten good at playing the game he wanted me to play. Whenever he accused me of anything, I became very affectionate and showed him that he was the only man for me. I cooked for him and made him feel at home in my apartment by giving him a key. My focus was on surviving so whatever it took I did. I can safely say that I never used drugs even though I am sure Dwayne asked me too. However, he never smoked around me or Alice.

In Summer 1998, I was now in my senior year of graduate school. At this point I had the option to graduate that year or to add another year for research. The research would take me home since my thesis was based on the educational system in the Bahamas. Yes, this was my way out! Hence, I extended my time by adding on the additional year. I didn't tell Dwayne about my decision. When the time came for me to start my research was when I told him. I got rid of everything I had in my apartment. I sold some of my furniture, and gave the rest of them to Janice and her daughter. I packed up my clothing along with all of my toddler's items and returned home to Nassau, Bahamas. I got no fight from Dwayne. I was free! Well so I thought.

Chapter 7: "Breaking Free!"

Returning home to the sunny island of New Providence was such a joy and brought me such comfort. It was great seeing my family again and being away from Dwayne. I didn't know how to feel now that I didn't see him every day. It felt like a dream. Could I really be free of him or was this just wishful thinking? My daughter was growing up so fast and it was almost time for her to start pre-school.

Dwayne would call on occasion to check on her but I knew it was an excuse to talk to me. Without even asking, he would tell me that he was leaving his wife so that we could be together. His words were as empty as a barrel to me now because I had heard all of those lies before. I would brush him off and end the call with some lie until the next time when he would start his foolish talk all over again.

Standing up to him was new for me but it felt good. I think he realized that I was slipping away because he had gotten use to just saying he missed me and I would come running back to him. Well, not this time. I was tired! Have any of you ever gotten so tired until your brain was tired? Well, that was my kind of tired. Dwayne realized that his words meant nothing to me anymore and I guess he couldn't handle that. I thought this man was finally realizing that it was time to give up this game because I was no longer biting but he decided to invade my space by visiting Nassau.

I was living with my little sister Jewels at the time so there was no way he was going to stay there. In fact, I was in shock when he told me that he was coming for a visit. I was like,

"Ummm, visit? Where? Why?" I was confused.

I thought I was being clear about my request but he wanted to talk. He wanted to explain to me how much I meant to him (So he said). There was nothing I could do to stop him from coming so he came.

He met me at my parents' house. We sat there for a while but I was a bit nervous seeing him because all I could remember was what I had gone through before. At that moment, I really felt confused. Moreover, I found myself experiencing a myriad of emotions. What should I do? He wanted to talk to me alone. I started to get scared but I told him that I would have to borrow someone's car so that we could go somewhere quiet to talk.

"Lord keep me safe." I prayed.

Reluctantly, I went for a drive with him. After driving around for a while with him not saying much of anything, we went to my sister's house. No one was home so we had the quiet space he wanted for us to talk. After about five minutes of him not saying anything that made sense, I realized that he really didn't want to talk after all. He wanted sex. Wow! He travelled all this way just for sex. Really? I guess he found the girl who could scratch the itch after all!

Even though I told him no; he didn't take no for an answer. I really didn't want him to rape me so I gave in. After it was over; I still felt like I was raped. I felt so dirty and used. Once I got dressed, I jumped in the car to leave and he followed. We went back to my parents' house with no conversation. I just wanted him to go away.

He came by my parents' house as often as he could after that. His trip that was supposed to be brief, kept being extended until months had passed. I really didn't know where he was staying and never asked. Apparently, he had rented a place because he was always well dressed and well fed. He seemed to have a substantive amount of money too so business must had gotten better since I left.

In September 1998, I started working at a pre-school in walking distance of Jewel's house. I liked the job a lot but I started to feel sick a week after starting. I thought I had caught a stomach bug but when I looked at the calendar, I noticed that it had been about two months since Dwayne and I had sex.

"Oh, no! Say it isn't so," I said to myself.

I couldn't believe that I was about to walk this path again. Panicked, I bought a pregnancy test, took it and lo and behold; it was positive! I was too sick to be upset with myself and remained sick for about a month or two. This baby was not allowing me to keep any food down. I was trying hard to not get fired from my job due to my constant vomiting.

Finally, the bad feeling subsided and I started to feel normal again. I continued to work on my research while working which was going very well. I didn't own a computer at the time so thanks to my friends who owned computers, I was able to type my thesis on the weekends and in the evenings.

Life was going well for me even though Dwayne was still in the country. I was hesitant to tell him I was pregnant but I did. Since I told him this, he tried hard to prove to me that he was serious about me but it was not working. I had been on my job for six months which allowed me to save some money. It didn't take long before I got an apartment for Alice and me to move into then lo and behold, Dwayne suddenly had nowhere to live. Like seriously?

I can remember while I was waiting for the landlord to paint the apartment that I stayed at my parents' house. One-night Dwayne was there very late so my mother asked me why he wasn't leaving. She insisted that he had to leave before my father got home. I told Dwayne that. It was at that moment that he stated that he had to leave the place where he had been staying because his time there had expired. I told him that this is not my house so he had to ask my parents' permission to stay the night. My father agreed for him to stay.

Somehow my father took a liking to Dwayne. I don't know why, how, or when but he did. My father had no idea of the amount of drama I was going through with Dwayne. I did a great job keeping it a secret from both my parents. Dwayne was a manipulator so he knew how to feed you the information he wanted you to know and to withhold the bad.

He also knew how to turn situations around to make you the bad person and him the savior. I believe that he painted a picture to my father that he was this good guy who meant me well. I am sure he never told my dad that he had a wife, hit me, tortured me, threatened to kill me, called me horrible degrading names or had sex with me against my will. I am certain of that!

When I moved into the apartment a week later, Dwayne didn't move in right away. I didn't want him to move in with me, hell, but I acknowledged that he would be homeless just like I was in Atlanta so I showed him some compassion and allowed him to sleep on my sofa. I knew what he was doing. He was trying to weasel his way back into my life. I felt like screaming because I knew myself very well and acknowledged that if he stayed there long enough that we were going to be intimate.

Once Dwayne got there, he did everything he could to woo me. He made sure he bought or cooked my favorite foods, he cleaned the house, he took care of Alice, and bought things that were needed with the little cash he had left. I almost felt obligated to reward him with a little bit of me. Since he was going to be staying here, I told him that he needed to get a job. Knowingly, I understood that he had no work permit which would pose a problem so I gave him advice on what he could do to contribute to the household. I don't know what he did but he was doing something because he started contributing to the household.

In May 1999, I started to prepare for the arrival of my second child. I didn't know if I was having a boy or girl but had suspicions that I was having a boy. Why? Well, this pregnancy was totally different from the first one which made me believe that this baby would be of the opposite sex. Never-the-less, I kept my options open. I went into labor on May 9. I went to the maternity ward after the pain started but they sent me back home saying that I had not dilated as yet.

I remained in pre-labor the entire day. The pain was so severe that I felt like I was going to die. Everything I ate I vomited back up or passed through my bowels. Nothing was staying down. This baby did not want food; it wanted out! I am thankful to Dwayne for being there because he helped me greatly through the pain and agony of that day.

In the wee hours of the morning of May 10th, the labor pain got so bad that I went to the hospital again. When the nurse checked me, I had finally started to dilate so I was admitted. It didn't take long before the pain got more intense. I was in labor for approximately six hours which seemed like an eternity.

I had no insurance so I had to endure the agonizing pain of labor and delivery without medication. There are no words to explain the pain that I felt that day but I thank God, I had a healthy baby boy! My baby looked just like his father. At the time, I didn't know how to feel about that because Dwayne and I were no longer in a relationship. It was complicated.

I was so happy to finally be home with my son – Drew. Alice loved her brother so much that she was like his personal bodyguard. Whenever he was in his bassinet she sat on the bed watching him sleep. As baby Drew grew, he started to look more like my brothers which was good.

My focus was so much on Drew that I didn't even realize that Dwayne was changing. He started becoming more irritable and anxious. I figured he was just tired because he had started recording music in the living room of my apartment which kept him up late.

Around that same time, my oldest brother Alex started asking me about Dwayne. I didn't think anything of it. I just thought he wanted to learn more about him and what he did so I candidly answered his questions.

About a year later, as we were preparing for my sister Brenda's wedding Dwayne had his first incident with Alice. She was about three years old and Drew was one. She had done something that was to me trivial but Dwayne was so upset by it that he decided to beat her. I told him that I would handle it but he started to show me that face again that looked like he was possessed which made me afraid so I stepped back. I didn't expect him to do what he did.

He took my child into the bedroom and beat her to the point that Brenda who was visiting was afraid. All we heard were screams that penetrated deep within your soul. I knocked on the door and told him to open it! He didn't. I knocked on the door more forcefully then he finally opened it and I got my daughter. My child was frightened!

How could he beat her like that I wondered to myself. Well, my sister didn't care. She told him that he was mean and heartless to scold a three-year-old like that. She pissed him off so much by what she said that he left. I don't know where he went but by the time he got back we were all asleep. Brenda's wedding was a few days away so we needed our beauty sleep. I was so angry with Dwayne that I could "kill him!" However, I kept Alice away from him as much as possible.

Sometime later, Alex approached me again about Dwayne telling me that he had been seeing him with some questionable persons in the neighborhood. He didn't go into detail but he was so concerned that he told me that I should ask Dwayne to move out of my apartment. Even though Dwayne and I were not together like we were before, we were together. We slept in the same bed and exchanged favors which I guess was acceptable for both of us at the time.

However, I was starting to get concerned about his behavior because he was leaving the apartment late at night and coming back hours later. This may sound strange but I didn't mind when he was gone because the unit was quiet, yet at the same time I wondered where he was going and what he was doing.

Over time, his nightly outings became more frequent and at times he would return with a brown paper bag. I didn't know what was in the bag because he usually hid it. One time when he got back to the apartment, he left the brown bag in the kitchen on top of the refrigerator so I looked in it. It had a bottle of vodka and a small foil packet. I didn't open the foil but I knew what it was. Dwayne was using drugs.

I knew from experience not to approach him about it because he would get belligerent so I went to my brother and asked him what he knew about Dwayne's involvement with drugs. It was at that moment that my brother explained to me that

Dwayne was not only using marijuana but he was mixing it with cocaine. To add, he stated that Dwayne was drinking some hard-core substances such as gin and vodka. This information confirmed for me what was in the brown paper bag that I had peaked into previously. I was shocked! This was frightening because I had children in my home who this man could harm while high on drugs and alcohol. He had to go!

The last straw for me was when Dwayne did the unthinkable. Alice was now in K-4. I was running a bath for her so that I could get her ready for school. Dwayne had just gotten in from where ever he was. He insisted on giving Alice a bath. I said no for a number of reasons but he insisted. I told him that it wasn't necessary. He got loud and aggressive so I stepped back. I was scared because I could tell that he wasn't himself.

He got through giving Alice a bath but as he took her out of the bathtub, he pulled her out by her arm and dislocated her shoulder. All I heard was a loud scream. When I got into the bathroom, my daughter's arm was hanging. I screamed, grabbed my child and ran to the phone to call my father for a ride!

I didn't have a car at the time so I needed a ride to get to the emergency room. While I waited for my father to get there, I chewed into Dwayne. I asked him what the hell was his problem? I asked him if he realized that Alice was four years old! Do you know what he told me?

"I didn't realize that I pulled her with such force. I'm sorry," he responded.

I didn't want to hear it! While crying, I asked him why he felt it was fine to pull her out of the tub by her arm anyway? He had no answer. I was so furious that I knew that this was it for me. I no longer felt safe with him around me or my children.

My father came right away and took us to our family pediatrician. I was terrified because I thought my daughter's arm was broken but her shoulder was dislocated. I felt like killing Dwayne and by the look of horror on my father's face; he wanted to kill him too! The doctor tried to calm us down and told us that he had to snap her shoulder back in place. He stated that it would hurt but once he snapped it back in place, the pain would lessen.

That didn't make me feel any better because all I could see was my child hollering in pain on that bed as he and the nurse held her down to snap her shoulder back in place. Thank God it only took one time for her shoulder to snap back in place because I could not take any more of the screams from my child. She screamed so much that she had lost her voice. I was devastated with fear!

The atmosphere in my house was intense from that day on and I don't even know if Dwayne ever realized how serious what he did really was. Alice was afraid of her father but he was still her father. However, I knew that I had to have the conversation with

Dwayne and ask him to leave. It took me a few weeks before I built up the nerve to ask him to leave. I had to be strategic about it though because I was dealing with a paranoid, possessive, violent man who was usually under the influence of some drug or alcoholic beverage! I did not need him staying in my apartment after I asked him to leave so when I asked him to leave; he had to leave immediately!

The day finally came when I was going to ask Dwayne to leave. I don't know if he felt it coming but I can say this, the weeks leading up to that day were cold. He was sleeping on the sofa and he had not touched me in weeks; even before the incident with Alice. When I say this, I mean that I had lost all feeling for him. I no longer wanted him around me. It didn't matter to me if he was seeing someone else or not. I was done!

I waited until he returned to the apartment one evening to ask him to leave. I didn't even let him come inside. I had a friend there as back up just in case he decided to attack me. When he arrived, I told him that he was no longer welcomed here so he had to leave. I also told him that I had called the police so he had to leave right away before they got here.

He was furious and I could tell that if I didn't have a friend there that he would have hurt me. He took his stuff that we had packed and reluctantly left. I don't know where he went and honestly; I didn't care. He had been in Nassau long enough to have met some people and made some friends.

Even though Dwayne was gone and I was now free of him; he was still in my head. The fear remained because that look he gave me was one of hatred. I saw the evil in his eyes. I was convinced that Dwayne had demons. I don't know how many but if I was a betting woman; I would say a lot.

That night he returned and tried to break into my apartment. I was scared for my safety and that of my children so I called the police. They came and checked the property but he was long done. Dwayne never returned to the apartment after that night.

Chapter 8: "No More Scales on My Eyes!"

I remember the way I felt after Dwayne left. I was finally free and I knew it! Weeks had passed and no Dwayne so the reality of me being free became more apparent every day. My father had purchased me a car so I was so happy to have transportation.

It was great to have my joy back and to feel carefree! I was driving one day as I ran some errands for work then as I sat at a red light, my vision became clearer. I could see the brightness of the sun for the first time in what seemed like years. It was like the scales had been removed from my eyes and suddenly I started to see things I could not see before.

This was the moment when I realized that for the past seven years I had been living a lie. I can't begin to expand the anger I felt. Subsequent to me being free from Dwayne, I now had to face myself. I had a decision to make. How do I get past all of the hurt and pain that I had bottled up inside for all of those years? I had no answers. All I knew is that Dwayne was gone and I was happy to still be alive.

I started to believe that my children and I could have a great life. I had graduated from college with my Master's Degree and gotten a great job. Alice was now in grade one and Drew was in K-2. We still lived in the same apartment which was peaceful now that Dwayne was gone. I hadn't seen him in months so I honestly couldn't say if he was still on the island or not.

When I dropped my children to school, there were certain routes I took to avoid traffic and others I would utilize when I collected them every day. One sunny afternoon as I was on my way to pick Alice up from school, there he was-Dwayne- standing on the corner staring at me. I was stunned and scared at the same time. I continued driving, got my daughter then went home. The next day, there Dwayne was standing on the corner as I dropped my son to pre-school.

"What was he doing? I thought. "Was he stalking me?"

For the next few weeks, this man followed me every day and made sure that I saw him. He knew my every move.

"How could he know this?" I wondered.

Little did I know, he had been secretly following me for the past few months then when he felt he had mastered my every move, he decided to fill my life with fear; this time from another angle by stalking me. I was so disturbed because my peace and calm had been shaken by his sporadic appearances on the street corners he knew I frequented throughout the day. I never knew which corner he would appear on or when. He would just show up which terrified me. I felt like I was in a dream. I became very paranoid!

To make matters worse, he started calling my home threatening to take my children out of the country.

"Oh no! Not my children, Lord please!" I prayed.

I got so scared that I contacted the police and The Department of Social Services to find out what to do. They could do nothing to help me so I wrote each of their schools a letter asking them to not release my children to anyone other than me or the names of the persons on the letter. I also forbade them to release them to their father due to his violent nature. Both schools honored my request which gave me some degree of comfort.

Dwayne followed me every day without fail and I can tell you that even though I was terrified, I determined in my mind that this had to stop. I can't remember praying much while I was with Dwayne but somehow, I felt the need to pray then. I knew that this man was trying to break me down at all costs and he was winning. I had to pray and call upon the name that is above all names; the name of Jesus Christ! I needed courage to face this man for the last time.

I was feeling so beat down and run down after ducking and dodging him for weeks that I decided that now was the time to confront him. Instead of waiting for him to roll up on me, I rolled up on him. Once I got there, I immediately put the car in park in the middle of the street and jumped out. I was so fed up that I told him some choice words that I dare not repeat verbatim, but in no uncertain terms I told him the following:

"I am tired of you following me, scaring me and trying to intimidate me. It is over; get it through your thick skull that I am done with you! Do not follow me anymore, do not come by my house and do not call me anymore. If you follow me again I will run you over and break both your legs! Do I make myself clear?"

I didn't wait for a reply. I jumped in my car and sped off. I never saw him again from that day. He was finally gone! Now I could say that I was finally free of Dwayne.

Shortly after that, my children and I moved in with my parents. That Christmas, Dwayne appeared like Santa Claus and left gifts on the porch for my children in the wee hours of the morning. I opened the door as he was leaving and told him not to start something he can't continue so as to not disappoint my children. He didn't listen and left the gifts.

The following Christmas and all those to follow he didn't remember my children at all. Can you guess what he was trying to do? He was using Christmas gifts as a wimpy attempt to win me back. When he saw that it didn't work, he forgot about his children permanently.

As dirty as Dwayne's final game was, my children didn't miss him. They were so happy and so well taken care of that they wanted for nothing. My children were in private school, they had the best of everything and most importantly, they were showered with lots of love. For the next two years, life was the "best they had been ever!" I found myself enjoying life in a way I never had before.

Chapter 9: "Break Out!"

The next two years after I broke free from Dwayne were my make-up years. For seven years of my life I was in bondage at the hands of a man who claimed to love me. These were the years in my early twenties when I should have been having fun and enjoying my life. I can't say that I regretted my decisions because if I didn't meet Dwayne, I wouldn't have my two beautiful children who I love immensely. Many people would not understand what I am saying but I hope some of you do. A mother's love is stronger than any other human form of love. It is so strong that the love of a man cannot replace it. Well, in my book anyway.

I was now living in an apartment with my children. Every weekend, I found a party or event to attend. I was making up for lost time. I was fit and slim so I could wear anything I wanted. I wore my hair short with beautiful colors in it which I kept well groomed. When I went clubbing, my children stayed with my parents. I was not in a relationship and liked it that way. I was not allowing myself to think about what I had experienced with Dwayne. All I wanted to do was have some long overdue fun!

My girlfriend Pharra and I spent a lot of time together. We were friends since high school. We were two of the smartest girls in school but I was more reserved and she was out going. She had grown up to be what you call a high maintenance girl. She knew how to get what she wanted from men without giving up "the cookie." I was learning from her but I quickly learned that this was not the life for me. I really could not swing guys out of money, name brand handbags or jewelry. It just didn't seem right to me so I didn't do it.

However, Pharra was making it big time by running games on men. She also taught me how to dress for the clubs because I was out of touch in that area. Hanging out with her made me feel alive! We remained clubbing buddies for the next year. However, that had to change when I got a new job with the educational system.

I loved the job I had but there was a part of me that wanted to work in the school system so I had applied for a school counseling job. Sooner than expected, I got called in for a job interview and was hired. I was elated! With this new career opportunity afoot, I decided to make some changes to my life style.

I made a promise to God that once I got this job that my life would be available to Him and that I would make my life an open book to my students. That meant that I had to become transparent. I had to be prepared to face my own demons in my closet which I had been running away from since Dwayne left. I don't know if I was ready for this move but it was too late. I had already made the promise and I am a woman of my word.

As I got ready to start my new job, I changed the color in my hair to black and I bought clothing that was conservative and student friendly. I wanted students to see me as professional yet friendly, approachable, and helpful. I wanted my new colleagues to view me as a professional too, after all I had a Master's Degree.

I started the post in the last term of the school year which was the last three months of school. This was a beautiful school but the atmosphere was not right. It was cold and the air was thick. I quickly learned that there was some division between the teaching staff and the support staff over space so the principal gave me the task of fixing the situation. I knew that God had placed me there for a reason. I knew that I had to get serious with my relationship with God and allow Him to use me to bring about change in that environment. This is when my life turned around and God began a work in and through me.

Section 3
Spiritual Awakening: Sold Out for Christ!

Chapter 10: "Self-discovery and Healing!"

I had come to realize that God had a call on my life. Once I stopped running, and stayed still long enough, God started to speak to me. I would feel the kiss of the Holy Spirit on my cheek every morning at 6:30am as He woke me up for morning devotion with Joyce Meyer. I didn't know it at the time but God was exposing me to teaching to help me discover who I was in Christ so that I could begin to heal.

As God woke me up, I was obedient and took notes from the programs I watched. The messages were so profound that I used some of them as I taught life skills to my students. Consequently, as I was teaching them, God was using the same information to teach me about myself and draw me closer to Him. In order for my life to really be used by God, I had to repent of my sins and become totally sold out to Him. That didn't happen right away as I was very much so wounded and broken, but it did over time.

After I gave my life to Christ, He became my life. I wanted to learn more and know more about Him. Everything I did was centered around God. I played nothing else in my office than gospel music. I was not a Christian fanatic but I loved God so much because I finally understood that it was Him who saved my life when I came face to face with death at Dwayne's hands. I could not help but love and praise this God who loved me so much to cover me with His shield of protection.

    I finally realized that I was searching for love when all the while the love of God was right there. I can't even explain the love I felt when I accepted Jesus as my Lord and Savior. This wasn't the first time I had accepted Jesus into my life. The first time I did, I was fourteen years old but I had been talking to God long before then. My conversation with God started when I was about nine years old.

    At the age of fifteen, I joined the Student Christian Movement at my high school when I met this young man by the name of Clayton. He too was a Christian and we became very close. He was my only male friend and if I can be honest, he taught me a lot about God at that age.

    I did not have anyone else around me at the time who I could talk to about God because my parents were strict which didn't leave any room for small talk or any talk for that matter. We grew up in that era when children were to be seen and not heard so that was still very much so embedded in me. I didn't know how to talk to my parents at that time anyway and my father and I didn't get along. Hence, Clayton was my lifeline at the time as a baby in the Christian faith.

    At the age of twenty-nine, I again felt like a baby Christian because I had not been in a committed relationship with God for a long time. This time I was older so I knew what I needed to do. I had to let God be my lifeline. From that day, God through the Holy Spirit guided me through my self-discovery period.

I learned about myself in ways I never had before. He showed me my flaws, He showed me my strengths, He showed me what threatened me and how He wanted to bless me and make me a blessing to those around me. I was on a journey of self-discovery. During this time, God spoke to me in dreams. I was dreaming about significant things that I needed to address to grow in Him.

He took me back to a time in my young life when I doubted him. I was around seventeen years old and studied the Word often. However, some of it confused me so I went to my pastor at the time for assistance. I took my questions to him and instead of answering me, he told me not to question God. I didn't understand why he said that. Could I not speak to God for myself? Would God be mad with me if I questioned the meaning of His Word or asked for clarification? I was confused.

This pastor left me doubting God and whether He was real when it wasn't God who had shunned me; it was man. This doubt followed me as I went off to school and opened the door for Satan to play with my mind by exposing me to other religions and leading me to a superficial kind of love that almost caused my demise.

could not help but love and praise this God who loved me so much to cover me with His shield of protection.

I finally realized that I was searching for love when all the while the love of God was right there. I can't even explain the love I felt when I accepted Jesus as my Lord and Savior. This wasn't the first time I had accepted Jesus into my life. The first time I did, I was fourteen years old but I had been talking to God long before then. My conversation with God started when I was about nine years old.

At the age of fifteen, I joined the Student Christian Movement at my high school when I met this young man by the name of Clayton. He too was a Christian and we became very close. He was my only male friend and if I can be honest, he taught me a lot about God at that age.

I did not have anyone else around me at the time who I could talk to about God because my parents were strict which didn't leave any room for small talk or any talk for that matter. We grew up in that era when children were to be seen and not heard so that was still very much so embedded in me. I didn't know how to talk to my parents at that time anyway and my father and I didn't get along. Hence, Clayton was my lifeline at the time as a baby in the Christian faith.

At the age of twenty-nine, I again felt like a baby Christian because I had not been in a committed relationship with God for a long time. This time I was older so I knew what I needed to do. I had to let God be my lifeline. From that day, God through the Holy Spirit guided me through my self-discovery period.

I learned about myself in ways I never had before. He showed me my flaws, He showed me my strengths, He showed me what threatened me and how He wanted to bless me and make me a blessing to those around me. I was on a journey of self-discovery. During this time, God spoke to me in dreams. I was dreaming about significant things that I needed to address to grow in Him.

He took me back to a time in my young life when I doubted him. I was around seventeen years old and studied the Word often. However, some of it confused me so I went to my pastor at the time for assistance. I took my questions to him and instead of answering me, he told me not to question God. I didn't understand why he said that. Could I not speak to God for myself? Would God be mad with me if I questioned the meaning of His Word or asked for clarification? I was confused.

This pastor left me doubting God and whether He was real when it wasn't God who had shunned me; it was man. This doubt followed me as I went off to school and opened the door for Satan to play with my mind by exposing me to other religions and leading me to a superficial kind of love that almost caused my demise.

As God revealed these things to me, yes I felt broken but as He revealed a flaw, he replaced it with his fruits of the Spirit (especially His peace, love and joy) which strengthened me. God made me smile every day because even though it was my job to empower and equip my students, He used the same information to heal me.

I don't know what my life would be like at this juncture if I did not commit my whole life to God. Once He had dealt with me at this stage of my life and gotten me to the point where He had stripped me clean, it was now time for me to do some work for Him. This entire process of self-discovery and healing took a year and a half.

Afterward, He opened doors for me to empower and equip students with skills that would help to usher them into their purpose even more. On this new path, I was redeployed to another island within the Bahamas where I had some very tough battles to fight for His kingdom.

To the natural eye, I was just doing my job as a counselor but in the spirit realm, I was fighting battles and war faring to save the souls of students who were being oppressed. One thing I learned about being sold out for Christ is that Satan gets angry and wages war against you.

Chapter 11: "Battling to Save Souls for Christ!"

I remember when my supervisor sent out the email letting us know that there were vacancies on other islands that needed to be filled. She told us that she wanted some persons to volunteer to fill the posts. I was not keen on going to a Family Island because I loved the schools where I worked.

I was now an Itinerant counselor responsible for three schools. I had opened the guidance offices at two primary schools in Southwestern New Providence and held sessions at a third school in the same district one to two days weekly.

It was hectic having this level of responsibility but I handled it well. In this position, I realized that being book smart and qualified were important, but to be effective, you needed to know Christ.

Over the first two years of my career, I had to call upon divine intervention to help students with various problems they were encountering, including the student who was being haunted by her deceased father. They don't teach you how to deal with that kind of case in university.

As I dealt with case after case, some of which pierced deep within my soul, I thought about my young children (who were then six and three) and ways that I could keep them safe from the monsters of the world including their own father.

The day came when letters of requests were needed for those interested in redeployment. One of my colleagues and I had already visited two islands so all we had to do was choose one, but I was undecided. Or was I? This could be the change I needed for me and my children; the change to better keep them safe. I felt this tugging from my spirit to write my request to go to one island in particular but I refused to write it. Instead I decided to go to bed.

Well, can I tell you that God and I had a wrestling experience that night because He would not let me sleep. My spirit was talking to me, telling me to write that letter and each time I refused. That went on for hours and even though I was sleepy; I could not sleep.

I was so tired fighting with God that I finally gave in and typed the letter. Can I tell you that once I typed that letter I fell fast asleep? God had an assignment for me on that island in the Northern Bahamas so I packed my bags and my two children and we moved.

I was actually excited about this turn of events despite my initial reluctance. I had no idea what to expect other than what I was told by the sitting Deputy Director responsible for redeployment at the time. He told me that the school that I was being posted to had no counselor and that there was a territorial war going on at the school. He told me that the school was divided by Haitians and Bahamians.

The problem didn't seem that bad listening to it but when I got there, I realized that this was a bigger problem than they could have ever imagined. Yes, the school was divided as stated and needed intervention from our superiors, but there was so much wrong with this environment that the grounds needed spiritual cleansing.

The school I was posted at was a high school; the only public high school in that part of the island. The population was under five hundred and the school catered to students from Grades 7 to 12. I remember trying to dialogue with the students at the school, but they were so closed off that it was hard to penetrate them. They let me know straight and plain that they didn't trust adults so I would have to prove to them that I was different. Need-less-to-say, I went about the business of earning their trust and many of them started to confide in me.

A series of events took place to bring healing to the environment including the first Student Forum that was ever held at the school. This event was held to give the students the voice they needed and felt they were denied, and to allow them to express themselves in any way they desired. It was a day for them to release all of the pain they had bottled up and to share their talents.

That was the day healing started on the school compound. Students became interested in learning again and as a result of intervention from our bosses, the teachers were now teaching again. I invited persons from various organizations to come in to speak with the students about scholarships and others to expose them to academic and career possibilities. Change had come to the school and a much-needed cleansing had begun.

This bold move did not come without a cost. Shortly thereafter, I was in a car accident which was meant to kill me and my children but thanks to heavenly intervention only the car died. We walked out of the car alive and no one understood how. Those who witnessed the accident knew that it was an act of God that saved us and that the accident was Satan's way of attempting to get rid of me.

The next morning when I woke up, I could not move. I was in so much pain that I had to call my cousin Debbie for help. I called my father for advice and he connected me with his lawyer. I was out of work for at least six weeks as I recovered, attended doctor in New Providence, and had x-rays done.

When I returned to work, many of the students who I had helped laughed at me and later some threatened to harm me and damage my new vehicle. Satan had waged war against me so I had to fight back. However, I quickly realized that I was in this fight alone.

As I fought to win the souls of these students, Satan came to my house, appeared in figures on my wall and even tried to get to me through my children but I anointed my children and myself with olive oil and kept God very much so alive in my life through prayer, fasting and praising.

Satan realized that he couldn't stop what I was doing so he worked through the teachers who rallied together to have me removed. They involved as many education officials as they could, including the union and even though I was removed from the school, God's will was still done. These people hated me because I was sold out to Christ. They hated me because I called them out on the wrong things they were doing and how they were short changing these brilliant students. I could not stand by and allow that to happen.

All I can say is that what Satan meant for harm, God turned it around for my good. No matter how bad this one experience was, I was able to touch so many students and save so many lives. Many of these students today are living their dreams and I know that I played a pivotal role through my obedience in helping them rediscover their skills, talents and passion so that they could fulfill their purpose.

Chapter 12: "Fake It Until You Make It!"

I was very disturbed that I had to leave my students at the high school. I had grown so attached to them and many of them to me. I was doing such a great work and the results were evident. However, I was transferred to the elementary school not far from the high school and the counselor from that school took my place at the high school. I didn't know how I would make it in this new environment because this wasn't where I wanted to be. To say I was hurt was an understatement. I was devastated!

In the coming weeks, I began to settle into my new school, doing my best to make every day a great one. I started to implement programs and visited classes to teach life skills. I could not understand why God had brought me to this island to bring me to a place of what I saw as shame. This made no sense.

As I visited stores in town, I started to see my students from the high school who were stunned to see me because they were told that I deserted them; that I didn't care for them after all. Can you believe the lies? I quickly dispelled the lies and told them exactly what happened and assured them that I was there if they ever needed me. They were so elated to know the truth; that I did not abandon them as they were told.

With this new information, I became sad because I didn't know how my students were being treated without me there to protect them. Every day was hard. Every day was a challenge but I learned to slowly let it go and trust God.

I remember speaking with a particular "first lady" of a local church who was on the compound for a visit. She told me that she had heard what happened and knew that the stories were not true. She told me that even though I didn't like what had happened that I needed to trust that God had a plan so until He revealed it to me, I needed to "fake it 'til I make it."

What was she saying? She was telling me that I must not allow the way I felt to dictate how I acted. I needed to take control of my feelings and do my work as unto God with joy and excellence.

From that day on that is exactly what I did. The weeks became months and the months became years and all was well. I actually grew to love the work I was doing at the primary school. My assignment had come full circle. I was now back at the foundational level of educational development to equip students with skills needed to better handle the challenges they could face at junior high school. God indeed had a plan.

Additionally, I was vindicated as the truth came out about what was going on at the school and teachers were being redeployed, retired and/or replaced on an annual basis. The superintendent was replaced for a more vibrant progressive one and the entire island started to make progress. It was wonderful.

Call it what you want but that was God completing what he had started. I was reminded of a scripture in the Bible that is found in I Chronicles 16:22 –

"Touch not mine anointed, and do my prophets no harm."

This verse has had such a profound impact on my life because every time someone rose up against me, God reminded me of this scripture and that He had me covered and not only that, but He had the final say!

While at this school, God opened the door for me to return to university to begin my doctorate degree. This had been a dream of mine since I was a little girl and now the opportunity came directly to my door. I didn't understand the reason for the move from the previous school to this one but God did, He knew that I needed to be there so that He could bless me for a job well done. Hence, I enrolled at Nova Southeastern University in South Florida, in Spring 2008.

SECTION 4
Vulnerability: Getting Weary in Well Doing!

Chapter 13: "Tears of Joy"

For the next six years, I remained on that beautiful island and was able to achieve so much not only professionally but spiritually. I had gone through a few relationships that didn't end well and was wondering if God was punishing me. I will admit that living for Christ is a lonely life and I had some weak moments.

One such weak moment resulted in me getting pregnant and in May 2009, I had a beautiful baby girl by the name of Olivia. I was so "much" in love with Olivia's dad that I was certain that we were going to get married but for some reason he was non-committal. I was so tired of being strung along that I broke off the relationship. I was heartbroken!

However, instead of allowing myself time to heal, I delved into talking to other men with hopes of meeting a nice guy who was ready to settle down and get married. A bad decision I would soon live to regret.

I joined a dating site and even though it was nice chatting with the men on there, it was a bit scary because you really didn't know if these men were who they said they were. Anyway, I was desperate so it was a risk I was willing to take so I went in on faith; or did I really. I talked to several men over the course of a few years and went out with several of them but there were no matches.

As I was about to give up and delete my account, one man in particular seemed nice. His name was Ronald. He lived in Nassau and had a job; praise the Lord!! Anyway, we started talking sporadically then more frequently as I felt more comfortable.

As we spoke, I felt as if he understood me and could relate to my frustration with men. I told him that I was looking for a relationship with a Christian man because my relationship with God was priority for me. He accepted that so we continued to talk. Little did I know, Satan heard my prayer too and etched a plan to entangle me with a wolf in sheep's clothing.

After talking for a month, we arranged to meet. I traveled to New Providence and he met me at the airport. I will honestly say that I was not thrilled when I first saw him but I went along with it. Ok; I am very picky. I am also attracted to what I see since I am a visual learner.

Hence, I have particular tastes when it comes to men which may be one of my major flaws. Anyway, I like men who are tall, dark and handsome. It almost sounds like a cliché, right? Well, there is more. He must dress well, smell good, and have a nice body. I like muscles, and a nice butt! It's nice to dream right? After, I got past my wish list, I realized that Ronald was just a normal guy with very few attributes from my list so I decided to go along with the plans for the weekend.

He rented a car for me to drive for the weekend which was sweet. Once I got the car, he left and returned to work and I went to my parents' house. Later that evening, we went to the movies which was nice. This man was not half bad. In fact, he was quite the gentleman. I could tell that he had so much pride being with me and I can say without reservation that it felt good to have a man put his arms around my waist. I was intrigued.

Once I returned home, we continued to chat online for weeks. The more we talked, the more I felt that he could be the one I was waiting for. His words seemed to hold a healing power and every time he spoke, I felt the hurt, pain, frustration, and disappointment literally peel away from my heart; I was beginning to let him in. Could this man really be the one that was sent from heaven just for me? I was starting to believe that he was.

We had been talking for six months and Ronald stated that he wanted to make me his wife. I was shocked and elated all at the same time. He told me that he was going to ask my father for my hand in marriage.

"What, men still did that?" I contemplated.

I felt blessed to have finally met a man who was prepared to treat me like the queen I knew myself to be. I didn't know when he was going to visit my father but I had a feeling that he was going to do it soon so I was excited. I knew that once my father gave his blessings that he was going to propose shortly thereafter. I was nervous because he was not prince charming but a very nice guy who gave all appearance that he would be loyal to and love me. As expected, my father gave his blessings.

It was not long after that when Ronald asked me to come to Nassau and we went ring shopping. The rings were beautiful. That Saturday was such a glorious day as we went from store to store viewing engagement rings and wedding bands. I always knew that I wanted my birthstone as my engagement ring so we looked at those ones first. He was supposed to get a regular white gold band but he decided that he wanted his birthstone in his band as well. That was a task because every store we went in either had very little men's wedding bands with his birthstone or none at all.

Once we got done with the shopping, we began talking about having an engagement party. Since I lived in the Northern Bahamas, the party would be held there in December 2013. It so happened that I got my final approval for my dissertation that month so I had something else to celebrate. I was now Dr. Samantha V. Evans. Wow! That sounded so good.

A whole lot of blood, sweat and tears went into me making it to this moment along with many sleepless nights and plenty of money. God is indeed good! I screamed though my house and cried for joy. What a huge accomplishment for a single mother of three! I couldn't stop singing praises to God that night. I think I disturbed my neighbors terribly but I was too overjoyed to care.

I had been living in my house for three years after going through so much stress to get it finished... but God! All I will say on this is that I went through three contractors to get my house finished. The first two in total stole about $30,000 worth of supplies and funds allocated for the completion of my house, resulting in me having to borrow an additional $20,000 for the third contractor to complete my house.

I moved into my house in February 2010; one-month shy of Olivia's first birthday. Even though I went through so much calamity with this major project, we were finally in our home so we were elated!

Our house is a modest-sized house with four bedrooms, two bathrooms, a living room, family room, office, dining room, laundry area and kitchen. It has an open floor plan along with a large back porch and a carport. Our house was full of love, laughter and peace. This house was built to be a family home where God and us would dwell and that is what it became.

Everyone who entered our home felt the warmth and love therein. We were happy; we were home. However, three years after we moved there, some wicked jealous people tried to chase me out of my home by sending evil spirits to my house.

Chapter 14: "Satan Initiates His Plan to Destroy Me!"

We were so happy in our home. My three children and I had so much fun making our house a home. My oldest daughter Alice was in grade twelve, Drew was in grade eight and Olivia was about four-years-old. When we entered our house, we knew that we were home and that God dwelled there.

We lived there happily for two years without incident but things began to change early in 2013. This was our third year in our home and my children were doing well. I had started my own business offering after-school tutoring to students in the community. Life was great! I guess I wasn't supposed to be this happy in my home because early that year, very strange things started to happen.

I first realized that something was wrong when I went home for lunch one day. As I passed my hall bathroom, headed to the master bedroom, I heard this double cough. My first thought was that someone had broken into my house so I quietly stepped backwards until I got to the front door then quickly jumped in my car and left.

I returned to my workplace and asked a male colleague to return with me. We walked through and through the house but could find no signs of a break-in or that anyone was there. I could not understand what was going on. Was I going crazy?

That evening when I returned home, I was a bit paranoid. However, there was no indication that anyone was in my house. I can say this though, I started to have difficulty sleeping. At that time only my son and youngest daughter lived at home. Alice was now living in New Providence with my parents.

My children were not being affected at that time; only me. The problems only occurred at night when it was time for me to sleep. It was like I was being tormented by something but I didn't know what that something was.

Additionally, I started to feel that I was not alone in the house. Whenever I went home for lunch, I was uncomfortable in my own home. I felt like I was being watched but I could not see by what or by whom.

I was becoming quite disturbed but I was too afraid to speak of what I was experiencing to anyone. It wasn't long until I realized that these were evil entities that were there to drive me crazy and that was not good. I knew the difference between God's presence and those of His angels; this presence was not them.

Once I figured it out, they got more brazen by inflicting fear on me and tormenting my mind so badly that I could not sleep without covering myself with protection scriptures. Even when I did, they would hold me down in my sleep so that I could not move and the only way I could free myself was by repeating scriptures in my spirit. I was terrified!

I didn't know much about warfare on this level where I was battling demonic spirits in my home so I needed help. I did some research so I could learn about what I was dealing with and realized that I needed to cleanse my house.

For months I was under attack by these evil spirits. I didn't know what they wanted but again my Heavenly Father let me know that He had me covered. They could not harm me physically but they were surely tormenting my mind and affected my sleep.

I started searching for my cleansing items and quickly realized that they could not be found where I lived so when I had a break from work, I went to New Providence to purchase the items. I went to one of the local malls with my mother and I came upon a stall there. They sold incense, scented oils and other such items.

I went to the lady and asked her if she had any white sage. She told me yes. I had never used any type of cleansing herb before so I asked her how to use it. She explained what to do. I also purchased a cross and olive oil before returning home. Once I got back, I anointed myself and my children then we prepared for the cleansing.

Based on the information received, each of us would take part in the cleansing ritual. In case you were wondering, my children were aware of the evil spirits in our home. Olivia told me one day that something evil was in my walk-in closet so she didn't want to go in there and she never did. I was shocked because my baby girl was only four years old. How could she know about spirits in particular the evil ones? I knew that she was right because the spirits were concentrated mainly in my master suite which consisted of my bedroom, bathroom and walk-in closet. They were there for me.

The day came for the cleansing. Before starting, I placed a cross on all of the windows and doors from the inside and outside with my olive oil. We opened up all of the windows in the house. We started in my master suite. My son carried the Sword of the Spirit which is the Word of God (Bible), my baby girl the cross and I quoted the scriptures and saturated the house with the white sage. I commanded all evil presence to depart in Jesus' name.

As we walked from room to room, I knew that angels had us covered. This cleansing was so powerful because even my baby girl was commanding the evil spirits to leave. We did the cleanse three times.

After it was over, I went to my bedroom where most of the activities took place and I can remember this so clearly. I commanded all evil to leave one final time and told them that they are not welcome here; that this is God's house then suddenly I heard a rush of wind just leave out through my master bathroom window. The wind was so strong that the curtains in my bedroom flew-up in the air. Immediately, the room felt different. I can't tell you how many spirits left that day but it was more than one. However, all did not leave. There was one left and I could feel it. This one wanted to see me dead!

The fight was on. It was just me and this bad boy. I needed reinforcement to get rid of this one. All I could do at this time was pray and cover myself because this spirit was not leaving. I prayed in the spirit. I knew Satan's plan so I never prayed out loud. I asked God for one specific thing. I asked Him to lead me to a pastor who knew how to fight demonic spirits. I didn't have anything against any other pastors but I knew that only a specific type of pastor could assist me with this battle I was fighting.

Months went by and I continued to fight this awful presence in my house. I waited with anticipation for God to answer me but honestly, I was getting weak. I wasn't sleeping well so I was always tired. I even went to the doctor for medication to help me sleep which did not work. He prescribed Oxycodone but it was too strong. It made me feel like I was losing my mind so I stopped taking it.

This experience was one I had never encountered in my life so I was growing wearier by the day. However, I remained on the battlefield. There was no way an evil spirit was going to run me out of my house or cause me to lose my mind! I had faith in my God and knew that He was working on a plan to defeat this evil presence that Satan had sent to my house.

After about six months of battling this demon in my house, God lead me to a particular pastor. He was someone I knew. In fact, his church was not far from my house. He was having an event at his church for the youth one Saturday and I was invited to attend. I took my children there for the day.

While I sat outside the church, he came to sit with me. We talked for a while then in my spirit, I felt a need to talk to him about my situation. As I spoke with him, he interrupted me and said,

"My sister I have been battling demons for years."

I was shocked because he was not the person I expected God to send me to but as he spoke I realized that he was indeed the right one.

After telling me about his numerous experiences cleansing places and freeing people of demons, he arranged to come by my house the following week to assess the situation and rid my house of the evil I was encountering.

The day finally came when the pastor came to my house with his assistant. They walked the perimeter of the house first before they went inside. Immediately, he could tell me that someone did this. He said that they were jealous that I had moved into my house so they were trying to run me out.

He further explained that there were several spirits there but a few I had gotten rid of. However, one was left and this one was mean and strong. He told me not to worry that they would get this awful spirit out of my house and they did. From that day on, I never had any problems with evil spirits in my house. Confirmation for me was when my baby girl went into my bedroom and opened my closet. Her response was,

"Mommy, the evil isn't in the closet anymore. It is gone."

I was elated and our house once again became our sanctuary. I continued to cover our home with the blood of Jesus Christ.

Satan had been defeated and he was angry. He had failed at running me out of my home and destroying my mind so he tried to break me down another way. He went after my oldest daughter Alice who was living in New Providence with my parents. This was not the first time he went after Alice. He tried to introduce that sexual spirit to her at the tender age of fourteen through a young man of eighteen years old who wooed her to the point that he showed up to my house.

I can remember very clearly what happened the night before the incident. I was in a praise and worship mood; my spirit was at peace and I was just loving on the Lord. I went to bed at about 11pm, but was awaken by a voice that told me to get up. I opened my eyes and looked at the clock. It was about 1:30am and my hall light was on. I got up and opened the door and Alice's room door was open and so was the hall door which I lock at night. I slowly walked down the hallway. When I got to the end of the hallway, I noticed that my back door was open. I started to panic but remained calm. Once I got to the door and looked outside, there was this man outside on my back porch with my child about to engage in sexual intercourse.

The Lord could not have awakened me any sooner because I caught them right before anything happened. It was only God that stayed my hand because as many two by fours that were on my back porch, I could have hurt him pretty badly. The case became a police and court matter so I cannot discuss the details but that sexual spirit was trying to enter my daughter that night but God said NO and intervened!

This time now, I got a call from Alice saying that she was being attacked by something she could not see. Before the attacks started, she was acting strange. In fact, she was accused of being rude and belligerent to my parents. In her mind, she wasn't doing anything wrong. I honestly can't say if she was or wasn't wrong because I was not there. I could only state what my parents and sister Jewels told me. Shortly thereafter, Alice started getting physically attacked in her bedroom by some evil entity.

She told me that she was being kicked and punched in her stomach and she heard something jumping back and forth on the roof. She was always terrified. She and Drew had also seen a spirit in the house. She saw the dark figure standing in front of her bedroom door and Drew saw it walk pass the same hallway where her room was. Drew was only visiting so he was not as afraid, but I don't know how long Alice had endured these attacks (and sightings) before she told me about them.

Once she told me, I let her know that she needed to cover herself with the Word of God. I had purchased her a devotional book sometime back which she used sporadically so I told her that she needed to read it day and night and cover herself from satanic attack.

I contacted a friend for advice who gave me some scriptures to give her to read to protect herself. I was so angry that Satan had waged war against my child that I began fighting him in the spirit from my home. There was no way Satan was going to drive my child crazy. She was so afraid that she could not sleep. However, once she started reading the scriptures and quoting them as she slept she started to get relief. They helped to protect her as she slept or got paralyzed (hagged) by the evil entity.

Consequently, she needed reinforcement from her home front to get the entity out of the house. When she called me, I decided to encourage her to ask my mother for help. My mother was quite familiar with fighting evil spirits so I asked her if she had spoken to Grammy about it. She said no so I asked her to put my mother on the phone then I told her.

Immediately my mom, got her olive oil and went through the house with her Bible pleading The Blood of Jesus Christ and rebuking that evil spirit. I heard her tell that restless spirit that it was not welcomed there and to leave in Jesus name!

My mother was busy rebuking that spirit for a while until it was gone. However, Alice was still afraid so I told her that I was coming. Before I left, I told that evil presence that I was coming and dared it to show up on my watch.

"You disgusting devil chose to terrorize my daughter and thought that I would not fight back?" I exclaimed to that spirit!

People of God, I never backed down from a spiritual fight! When I arrived at my parents' house, I let that evil presence know that I was there and dared it to show itself.

I am sure I didn't have to make that announcement because it knew when I arrived but I did anyhow. I slept in the same room where my daughter slept and was being attacked, without incident or disturbance. However, Alice was uncomfortable in that room so I moved her into the spare bedroom. She had no further disturbance of that nature since then.

Chapter 15: "Getting Married!"

It was my dream to get married from I can remember. I was now in my early forties so I was beginning to think that marriage was out of my reach. However, meeting Ronald was a blessing because I could finally make my dream a reality.

Once my father gave him my hand in marriage, we started planning our engagement party. I did all of the planning for the event inclusive of the decoration. Even though I had already selected my bridal party, only two of them lived on the island where the event was being held. However, I had no help. I was on my own.

The day finally came for the engagement party and Alice was there. She helped me decorate the hall for the party which started at 7pm. My Matron of Honor arrived and greeted the people as they came. Even though her help was needed earlier, I appreciated the assistance she gave that evening.

We had a family photo shoot planned for 5pm right before sundown and hoped to capture some romantic shots with me and Ronald as well. Ronald, my children, and I, all wore white for the shoot. The photo shoot went well. I was very pleased with the photos. Right after the shoot, we went home to get ready for the engagement party. I wore pink and purple and he wore purple with black slacks. We looked hot!

When we arrived at the venue, my parents, children and friends were there. My family lives in New Providence so they were unable to attend. We got a warm welcome when we entered and I showed off my engagement ring. Ronald didn't tell me which ring he had chosen so I didn't see it until he presented it to me earlier that day. It was a gorgeous white gold ring that had 2 karats emerald affixed. I was so overjoyed!

The evening was beautiful but clearly there were some skeptics in the room who questioned whether we were sure that we were right for each other. I found this question quite bizarre. Even though this was odd, I answered their questions, enjoyed a relaxing evening in the company of those present then went home feeling blessed and highly favored.

We had less than four months to plan this exquisite island wedding. Again, this was a challenge because contrary to the roles of the bridal party, my matron of honor was not as supportive as expected. In any event, the plans had to be made and executed.

If that wasn't enough, I had bridesmaids who stepped down and Ronald had difficulty getting persons to stand as his groomsmen. Looking back, I wonder if all of these challenges were not signs from heaven to run! To add, when we started counseling, Ronald revealed that he was uncomfortable with the fact that I was more educated than he was, which made me consider calling off the wedding. However, after we spoke, he didn't want to call it off so we proceeded.

To not go into all of the details of the wedding preparations, I can say without reservation that I found out who my friends were and who were really happy for me. I was very disappointed because I had to pay for the majority of the expenses associated with my bridal and lingerie shower which is unorthodox.

I was very hurt that those persons who I regarded so highly as friends didn't see fit to show their support on such a glorious occasion as this. As I reflect back, I wonder if this too was not a sign from heaven to run! In any event, the wedding plans continued.

The eve of the wedding came and again there were challenges. Ronald had indicated that none of his family would be able to make it there for the wedding so no transportation was arranged to get them from the airport to the wedding site nor were reservations made for them at the resort where all of us were staying.

However, lo and behold, a group of his family members arrived on the island that evening as we were preparing to go to our last practice at the church. This caused a whole slew of problems which were dropped in my lap yet again. The stress associated with this wedding was beyond any I had ever experienced before. Despite my careful and meticulous planning, there were unexpected and unforeseen problems every step of the way. I was in no way, shape or form a calm bride. In fact, my sister Brenda called me bridezilla.

The day of the wedding arrived and when I thought all of the problems were behind us; another one arose. Ronald's cousin arrived at the airport on the first flight which landed around 7am that morning, while I was getting favors and table toppings packed and ready for my very special day. Who do you think had to pick her up from the airport? Me! Why? Because no one knew she was coming so again no plans were made to transport her to the resort and I was the only one left in town with transportation.

Need-less-to-say, I graciously picked her up and took her forty-five minutes away to the resort. After dealing with this unforeseen event, I finally made it to my suite to get ready for my 2pm wedding. At that point, the only issues that surfaced were regarding the venue which my dear friend and assistant Kammie took care of. She was indeed Godsent for me that day.

The wedding was beautiful as I wore a white mermaid silhouette dress with lace and beading across the top and back of the torso. I was a gorgeous bride. My bridal party wore pastel spring colors with beautiful floral arrangements inclusive of roses and orchids. My bouquet consisted of orchids and an array of spring flowers which was breath taking. My groom wore a rose boutonniere and his groomsmen wore boutonnieres which matched what the ladies wore. My three children stood in the wedding. I was ready to say good-bye to the single life and become a wife.

During the ceremony, there was a section where Ronald made a commitment to love my children as his own and we lit a family candle. He also presented each of my daughters with a cross necklace and my son with a cross rosary. Besides birthing my children, this day was the most beautiful event in my life.

However, if someone would have pre-empted this day by saying that the wedding ceremony and reception would have been the best parts of my marriage; I would have rebuked them. However, after I got married, Satan came home with me.

Chapter 16: "Satan Came Home with Me!"

After a full day of wedding activities – the ceremony and reception – we were exhausted. However, I still expected to have a great honeymoon, but it did not go as expected especially since I had waited so long to be intimate with my husband. I chopped it up to him being tired but I was ready to have the wildest sex with him. No matter how hard we tried, he could not get himself together to please me the way I needed him to. Need-less-to-say, I was disappointed beyond words. The remaining days in the suite were similar but I was happy to be married.

After staying in our beautiful suite at the resort for three days, we returned home. I was happy to be a wife and looked forward to spending the rest of my life with my husband. Immediately when we arrived home, my son traveled with my father back to New Providence since school was on a week's break. Ronald and I enjoyed our first few weeks at home, basking in each other's company. Five-year-old Olivia was there with us. She was happy to have a stepfather especially since she barely saw her biological father.

My son returned a week later for school. I was happy to begin our life as a family. Ronald and I had done such a phenomenal job planning our wedding that I was excited to see what else we could accomplish together as a team. I looked forward to our future with great anticipation. I did have one concern though; we were not having sexual intercourse as I believe we should have been as newlyweds. In fact, whenever I initiated sex, he was always tired. I didn't think anything of it at first but his tiredness started to become the norm.

He told me that since he had to get up early for work and got off late in the evenings that all he wanted to do was sleep. I didn't push. Instead, I decided to spice things up in the bedroom by wearing sexy lingerie to bed. I had gotten many nice pieces in a multitude of colors as gifts so I took the opportunity to wear them to bed but that didn't work.

It didn't matter what I did or what I wore, this man was not interested in sex. I even went to bed barely cloth and he would not touch me. I was confused! I wondered what kind of man I had married. I did notice, however, that he was up between the hours of 2am and 4am every morning which I didn't question at first because he had to catch an early boat to get to work. Our sex life was nearly non-existent for newlyweds. I was unhappy and sexually deprived.

Two weeks after we got married, I started having pain in my abdomen. I didn't know what the pain meant but it felt like very bad cramps. I would be lying if I said the pain didn't concern me because it was intense but there was a part of me that had hoped that I was pregnant because I was ready to have another child. For the next month, I did not mind enduring the pain if this meant that I was going to be pregnant. The pain was bad during the day but it was worse at night. The pain was so excruciating that most nights I asked Ronald to rub my stomach to console me; which he did.

About a month after Drew returned home, I started having an issue with my laptop. One day, I went on my computer to do some work and a whole lot of explicit sites popped up of the pornographic nature. I was mortified! Immediately I blamed my son but he denied that it was him. To clear himself of my accusations, he quickly pulled up the history of the activities on the computer.

To my surprise, all of those pornography sites had been accessed while Drew was either asleep or away. That only left Ronald because I knew that it was not me or my five-year-old. I immediately confronted Ronald who tried to blame Drew but once the dates and times the sites were accessed was revealed he confessed. I was stunned! Why would a man who had just gotten married and had a sexy beautiful wife sleeping on the side of him every night desire to watch pornography? I felt so disrespected and disregarded.

It all started to make sense. Ronald didn't want to have sex with me because he was addicted to porn. Based on the history on the computer, he started accessing pornography from he arrived there for the engagement party. I felt so humiliated and lied to! We had agreed that we would not engage in any type of sexual activities until we got married so our contact was limited. However, I didn't know that he was pleasuring himself with porn and the filthiest of porn too! This made me wonder what else he was doing but I had no reason to accuse him so I didn't.

I was so distraught that I made an appointment to seek counseling at the church where we were married. I told the pastor what was going on and that I had no idea what to do. For the first time, I cried inconsolably as the reality of what I was facing finally sunk in. I was ready to walk away because I refused to remain in a sexless marriage where I was unhappy.

I even asked the pastor if there was any way our marriage documents had not been filed so that I could stop the process and just tear them up. He told me that more than likely they were filed. He convinced me to give it a chance to work out. I agreed to give it six months. He called Ronald to tell him my concerns and to find out what he desired to do. He agreed to attend counseling for the next six months. However, the only session he attended was the one that our marriage officer and current pastor picked him up to attend. He made no effort to save our marriage over this six-month period.

My birthday came near the end of May and he took me out for dinner which was very romantic. We needed an outing like that because our young marriage was suffering. That night, we had sex. He still had problems getting a full erection but something was better than nothing. However, Ronald refused to pleasure me orally nor did he want me to do that for him. I can clearly remember the words he said to me as I begged him to indulge me. He was mean.

"I don't do that," he said.

"What do you mean you don't do that?" I replied shockingly.

"You want me to die, aye" he shouted?

I was so hurt that I felt like just letting the ground open up and take me under. What man, real man, does not want to give his wife oral pleasure? Something wasn't right here. I wasn't getting regular sex and now there was no chance of me getting oral sex from my husband either? I couldn't believe what I was hearing. I felt so empty and unfulfilled. Who was this man I had married? I had never seen this side of him before.

Life for me became more difficult after that with my husband because sleeping in the same bed with him was very uncomfortable. I felt that this man did not love me. In fact, I was restless sleeping in my own bed. My spirit was cross (vexed) whenever he was in the bed with me. I felt like Satan was sleeping in my bed. I didn't know him anymore. He was different since we got married. This discomfort and evil presence were so unbearable that I moved him out of my bedroom into the spare bedroom. Finally, I was able to get some sleep again without feeling like I was in torment.

To make matters worse, the pain I was experiencing in my abdomen had gotten so bad that I went to the doctor for an examination and to take a pregnancy test. The doctor didn't find anything wrong and I was not pregnant. I can honestly say that I didn't believe the doctor because I was convinced that I was pregnant.

I took several other pregnancy tests independent of the doctor and they were all negative. Something was wrong. Even though my marriage was in jeopardy, there was a side of me that desperately wanted to be pregnant for my husband because honestly...I loved the man!

I decided to go to New Providence to visit my doctor so that I could prove that I was pregnant. When I got to Nassau, I went straight to the doctor for my visit. I was excited to get my pregnancy test so that I could see the positive reading. The doctor examined me and gave me a full physical; included in that was a pregnancy test. The test was negative again. I was devastated!

"I know I am pregnant," I explained to the doctor.

I asked him to take it again. He told me that if I said that I am pregnant again that he would call the Sandilands Rehabilitation Center to send "The Crazy Bus" for me because he would be convinced that I was crazy. I looked at him like he was crazy! He told me that he had some concerns so I had to get some tests done. I went to the lab for the tests and he sent my pap smear to another lab for reading.

I got back some of my results that same day. I was anxious but calm because my annual exams were always good. However, this time the doctor told me that my tests revealed some problems. As he spoke to me, I felt like I was in a trance. I felt like I was having an out of body experience as I could not believe what I was hearing.

He told me that I had three diseases; two of which could be treated with antibiotics but the other one required surgery. The doctor asked me who I had been intimate with and I told him that I am married so I had only been intimate with my husband. It didn't dawn on me at the time that I could have gotten sick from my husband. I was at a loss for words. I was in a daze for the rest of the day.

When I returned home the next day, I could not wait until Ronald got home to tell him what the doctor had discovered. I was in bed when he arrived home. He stood at my bedroom door and asked me what the doctor stated.

Once I told him, he didn't say anything. Instead, he walked away then returned and stood in the doorway of my bedroom as he told me that he knew why I was sick.

"How could you possibly know that?" I asked.

"I am the reason you are sick," he said. "I made you sick."

All I could do was look at him as many thoughts went through my head. Is he joking? Is this some sick game he is playing? Did this man just seriously admit to giving me three diseases? How the hell?? What the hell?? Oh, God! I immediately felt like I was going to die. I didn't know how to process what I had just heard. I was numb.

The following week was rough as I waited on the call from my doctor to get the results of my other lab tests including the sexually transmitted diseases. There are no words to explain the thoughts and feelings that went through my mind as I waited to hear if I had AIDS. The day came and I got the call. My entire body quivered with fear as I waited on the next end of the phone for the doctor.

Once he came to the phone, I believe that only the Holy Spirit kept me together and only my guardian angel kept me from falling off the chair as the doctor told me that all of my tests were negative. All I could say was thank you; oh thank you God!! I cried so much that day. Immediately I prayed and asked God for a way out of this marriage.

I told Ronald that I had to go back to New Providence to visit the specialist so that I could find out what I needed to do. He provided the money for the trip. I travelled a week later. After the consultation with one of the leading gynecologists and obstetricians in The Bahamas, he told me that I needed to have surgery immediately or my situation would not end well.

"What was I hearing?" I perplexedly thought. "What the hell was I dealing with?"

I cannot tell you how I dealt with all of this information other than God had me in the palm of His righteous right hand because I was nonreactive. I felt like I was living a lifetime movie. How did I get to this point? What went wrong? I had so many questions but no answers other than the ones Ronald had given me, and honestly, I no longer trusted him.

The surgery was very expensive but thank God I had insurance to cover 80% of the bill. I told Ronald that he had to pay the difference and he agreed. I had several trips after the initial consultation in preparation for surgery. Little did Ronald know that while in Nassau the week before the surgery, I had made an appointment to speak with a divorce attorney. I needed to know what the law stated about this cruel act that was done to me at the hand of this man I had married and how to legally get out of this mess.

Both appointments were on a Friday a few hours a part. The lawyer was shocked by what I explained. In fact, he thought I was lying. I told him that this is my life and showed him my documents from the doctor. He told me that he could file for early release due to cruelty and irreconcilable differences. I was prepared to do anything because I needed out of this marriage before this man killed me!

While in New Providence, Drew and Olivia stayed with Ronald. That was a huge mistake because this man mistreated my children. Drew called me and told me that Ronald didn't feed him; only Olivia. I asked him what he ate. He told me that he fixed something but Ronald had bought food home but only gave some to Olivia.

I had not gone to the store because I knew that I would only be gone for a few days. I also didn't expect Ronald to not feed my son. In my absence, he took this opportunity to bring contention into my home with an attempt of turning Olivia against Drew.

On Saturday morning, my son called me from his cell phone so that I could hear what Ronald was saying. I had given Drew instructions that morning to feed his sister and run her bath, then told him to ensure that she did some school work. Ronald was telling her not to listen to Drew and that she didn't have to do what he said. Drew told him that these instructions came from me. I heard this man say that he didn't care and instructed my baby girl to disobey her brother.

What further disturbed me was that Olivia was not talking to her brother, she was shouting at him. This was out of character for my daughter. Drew responded by telling her that mommy said to do this so you have to do it. Ronald then told my son to get out of my house. That was it! I told Drew to hang up the phone and that I would call Ronald. I told Drew to get his sister and walk to my friend's house around the corner.

I called Ronald on my house phone and asked him what was going on? He then told me that nothing was going on; that the children were fine. I told him that I was on the phone a minute ago and heard the entire discourse between him and Drew. He was so shocked that he could say nothing.

Subsequently, he got upset and said something stupid like he was going out so he wasn't going to be there to take care of my children. Now I knew that this man was weird but now he was just being stink.

"Ok, no problem!" I said. "I told Drew to take Olivia to my friend's house."

After our argument, I hung up and called my friend and told her what was going on. While I was talking to her, Drew and Olivia arrived at her house and she took care of them for the day. She fed them and cared for them in my absence. They were dropped home that evening once I confirmed that Ronald was there.

I can't even begin to describe the feeling of helplessness I felt at the hand of this man who was my husband. How could he mistreat my children? They came from me and will always be a part of me! The pain and anger I felt was a feeling so deep that if someone had cut me right then, I don't think I would have felt it or bled.

Ronald had done insensitive things like buy food only for me and him, and groceries for himself only but never had he been that cruel and not feed my son. However, it was becoming more and more evident that he disliked my son. I prayed for God's grace, mercy, self-control, and protection because there was no way I was going to have this man or any man mistreat my children.

I will say this now, ladies, no man should come before your children; ever! Step-fathers, don't you ever ask your wife to choose between you and her children. The children are not pawns for you to use to manipulate or control her. Ronald realized quickly that he was not number one over my children. God was first then my children then him.

I was all they had and for years they were all I had so there was no way he was coming before them. They are my heart; my soul; my life. I make no apology for that. God trusted me with these three lives so there was no way I was going to do them a dis-service by pushing them aside for a man.

SECTION 5
Matters of the Heart: Broken & Shattered

Chapter 17: "Stabbed in the Back by Family"

The weeks leading up to the surgery were very stressful. I was afraid to go "under the knife" per se but I knew that it was a necessity for me to free my body of the foreign matters that were there.

One Sunday afternoon after church, I was in Olivia's room cleaning up. I was feeling so tired and distressed then the phone rang. It was my older sister Brenda. I told her that I didn't feel like talking so she asked me what was wrong. I told her that I was going through something very difficult and private. She asked me if I wanted to talk to her about it and I said no, but she wouldn't take no for an answer.

After saying no several times, I told her that if I told her what was wrong that she could not repeat it. She promised me that she would not tell anyone so I told her.

My sisters and I grew up very close so talking to Brenda was normal because she is the oldest of us six siblings. Brenda and I are eighteen months apart so we were very, very close. She was like my heartstring and I consulted her for everything. She was my role model and I aspired to be just like her. Brenda was a brainbox-smart and sharp as a tack! In fact, she still is. She is a doctor today and doing very well for herself.

She looked out for me and I love her so much for that. While she was in college, I visited her often and we talked all the time. When it was time for me to start college, Brenda recommended the college that I eventually went to. She even came to Atlanta to help me settle in. When I enrolled in Nova Southeastern University, Brenda helped pay my tuition whenever I was short. She has always been a blessing to me and I to her so this madness going on here could have only come from the pits of hell!

I had not talked to Brenda as often as we used to and I could not give a good reason for it. I had just become a private person over the years. I love my privacy, but some of my family members are very free and loose with conversation. Anyway, after telling her about my problem with Ronald, she was upset naturally but I told her that it was going to be taken care of.

She asked me if I had confronted Ronald and I told her that I hadn't. Honestly, I was concerned about me at that time. I could always deal with him later. I also realized that I could not allow myself to get stressed out as I prepared for surgery. In any event, I was still so numb from the shock of this situation that I don't think anything could have gotten me upset.

The day before the surgery, I travelled to New Providence. Once I got there my daughter Alice called me into her room and asked me if I was all right. I told her yes. She asked if I was sure and I said yes.

"What is going on?" I asked.

She asked me why I didn't tell her that Ronald was hitting me. I was like,

"What? That man a'int crazy to put his hands on me." She then said,

"The news going around in the family is that he is beating on you and that he made you sick so that's why you having surgery to correct the problem."

I looked at Alice stunned and lost for words.

"Lord, what is this I am hearing today," I replied.

So Alice asked if it is true. I told her that I am having surgery because of him but he never hit me.

She was distraught and asked me why I kept it a secret. I told her that I was still trying to grasp it myself and didn't want to worry them. In fact, I asked her where she had heard these lies. She told me who she heard it from so I spoke to that person. That entire afternoon the drama unfolded and led back to Brenda who I had told about my stress a few weeks prior.

I texted Brenda with such anger in my words that if it was possible for me to make each of my words turn into nails that she would have been nailed permanently to the closest wall in her house.

"What part of do not repeat what I told you did you not understand," I shouted! Brenda swore that it was not her who had told our younger sister Jewels.

"You are a liar!" I responded enraged. "Why would you do this to me after I told you that this was a painful experience for me?" I cried!

It only could be her because I told no one else. She held fast to her story so I told her that I don't want to talk to her again.

Shortly after that I heard that Jewels was in a car accident. It was sad that that happened to Jewels but that is what happens when your mouth catches up with your deeds. It was a minor fender-bender (thank God) but it could have been avoided had Brenda respected my wishes and privacy. This betrayal hurt me to the core as I was stabbed in the back by my birth sisters!

These women are family but I wanted to just choke them for what they did to me. How could my sisters carry my name through the mud in such a way? I was devastated enough by what Ronald did, now between Brenda and Jewels they had me being beaten too. I had to catch myself and calm down because I had surgery hours away so I went by my youngest brother's house until I calmed down.

That day started turmoil in our family like never before. The tension between us sisters was thick. I could not trust them so I stopped talking to them. I even suspected that they were happy that I was suffering through this mess of a marriage. I never understood why they wanted me to suffer. I love my sisters so much but now we didn't have a relationship.

I had learned so much about how they felt about me, but had to swallow it and simply take it to the Lord in prayer because if I hadn't, the hurt from the pain would have consumed me. All I could say tearfully was,

"Jesus, you went to the cross for me and you did nothing wrong so I will bear this cross for being your servant child because I did nothing wrong to my sisters yet they defame my name!"

Conversation with them became very brief. I had forgiven them, for those of you who may be wondering, but we didn't talk, socialize, or share family successes or future dreams since then. They were almost dead to me. That is sad to say but it is very true.

The pain they inflicted on me with their words had ostracized me from them and it hurt my children. I became uncomfortable around them because I could feel that they had no good feelings towards me. Brenda had attempted to talk with me several times but I could not receive it at the time.

I didn't have conversation with them for two years. Then as God started to deal with me and prepare me for a deeper walk with Him, He told me that I had to strip myself of all un-forgiveness.

"Un-forgiveness," I wondered. "What un-forgiveness God," I asked?

As I was falling asleep one night in December, 2017, God showed me clear as day that I had not fully forgiven Brenda. He told me that I needed to make amends. I didn't question my heavenly father; I just did it.

I texted her on December 31st, and told her that I needed to talk to her. She messaged me back as I was getting ready for church so we didn't speak until January 1st, 2018. All I can say is that God led that conversation to a place of complete restoration that I never thought possible. There was less of me and more of God as we spoke. I even spoke with Brenda's husband because I felt compelled to mend that fence as well.

I now have a better understanding of what happened and realize that Brenda meant well by what she did but the information shared was blown out of proportion. However, I reminded her that I asked her to keep it confidential so she did betray my trust. She admitted to that and apologized which I greatly appreciated.

It doesn't matter anymore who said or did what. God has restored my relationship with Brenda and I am happy about that. He didn't lead me to talk to Jewels because I never shared any information with her, but only to release her to Him so I did.

I learned that you cannot make anyone love or accept you even if they are family. Some of them will support you and be proud of you while others will be jealous of every blessing that comes your way. Does that mean you treat them in kind? No! What it does mean is that you need to guard your heart, your mind and your soul against the enemy who can manifest himself through anyone; even family.

I decided to talk about this now because if my story can help someone then I want them to know how to heal their own heart from the hurt, hatred and jealousy of siblings or family, even if that means that you have to love them from a distance until God leads you to the place of restoration as He did for me!

Chapter 18: "Recovering from Surgery While Under Attack!"

Surgery day was a scary yet exciting day because even though the pain had subsided for the most part, I knew that I still had foreign matter invading my body that could possibly kill me if not removed so I willingly went under the knife. My doctor is one of the best in his field so I knew that I was in good hands. He told me that after the removal of all of the foreign matter that he will perform a D&C to clean out my system which I sanctioned.

The surgery was smooth and when I woke up I was comfortable. There was some pain which reminded me of the pain I felt after my C-section but less intense. I was discharged the same day but I could not drive for a week so I had to be picked up from the hospital. I stayed in New Providence for ten days as I recovered from the surgery. I can't recall being overly consumed with pain but I had medication to keep me comfortable until my follow-up visit.

While in New Providence, Drew stayed with Ronald which I didn't like but my son had to attend school. He did his best to stay out of Ronald's way which worked out well but he took to partying in my absence and chose to take Drew with him to Beer Fest in my vehicle; damaging my car in his numerous ventures. When I returned home, Ronald picked me up from the airport and took me home. He didn't know what to say to me but tried to engage in small talk. It was a strain to talk with him, however, I did my best to remain cordial.

Even though I was released to return home, I was not yet fully healed. Ronald did all he could to stress me out by just doing silly things in the house. He would parade through my house as if it was his, he stole money from me, he continued to complain about everything my son did and showed no interest in helping my teenage son grow into a godly young man.

I remember him going to the hardware store to purchase an item. While there, he brought a toy fishing rod for Olivia but got nothing for Drew. Of course, Drew asked him what he bought for him and Ronald bluntly replied, "nothing!" That really hurt Drew.

That night I started to have very bad pain and when I checked myself, I had puffiness in my cervix area and lower abdominal area where I had the surgery. It hurt so much that I soaked in Epsom salt to help relieve the pain. I soaked every evening until I could make it back to the doctor in New Providence.

I could not confirm it but I had a strong feeling that all of the stress in the house had hampered me healing at a normal rate. In fact, I had regressed some based on the intense pain felt in my lower abdomen and swelling felt in my vaginal area.

After all of this happened, I asked him to leave my house for the second time only to hear him say that he needed more time to find a place. I graciously reminded him that he said that the last time we spoke about him leaving and that his two months had expired.

As he walked away he stated that he has no family there so he needed more time. He went into the room he occupied and closed the door. Well, I was not hearing that. I had to seek God on this one because honestly, I couldn't take him being in my house any longer. This time, come hell or high water, he had to go!

The next day, while Ronald was at work, my son and I packed up his items, placing them in his duffle bag and a black garbage bag from the kitchen. We even fished his dirty clothes out of the hamper and placed them among the items packed. Yes, it was that serious folks!

I then placed them at the front door because he was not coming back into my house. I called a male friend and instructed him to inform Ronald not to return to my house. Instead, I asked my friend to come to collect his items and take them to him. Ronald was informed of this but him being the stubborn evil man he was, still showed up at my house.

Before he arrived, he texted my phone at least ten times. He was spewing out words of vile venom with one intent; to upset me. I was still healing from surgery and was already experiencing swelling in my groin and pubic area so I didn't need anything else upsetting me. However, he did not care.

He preceded to tell me that I cannot put him out of our marital home and that it was against the law. I didn't respond. Shortly after that, he texted and asked me to open the door for him. I did not.

He wasn't aware that I had the locks changed until he got there so his plan to invade my dwelling home was denied. A few minutes later, I heard a loud knock on the door.

"Open the door, this is the police!"
In shock I responded that I was in a shower. Once I got out of the shower, I got dressed and went to the door.

Once outside, I locked the door and told my son, who was fifteen at the time, not to open this door under any circumstances. I asked the officers if they wanted to speak here or go to the police station. They told me that they got a call about a domestic disturbance. My response to them was that I didn't make any call to the police station and that there was no domestic disturbance here.

The police then looked at Ronald who held his head down; proving that he was the culprit who made the call. I told them that only Ronald could say why he made this call. It was clear that the three officers; comprising of a sergeant, a corporal and a constable, were quite upset. The attention was turned to Ronald who was asked by the sergeant to explain himself. The sergeant spoke the following words to him:

"Sir, if your wife is saying that there is no domestic disturbance here then what is the problem?"

Ronald did not answer. The Sergeant further explained that they dropped other calls to come to attend to this situation which they deemed urgent. The sergeant asked him to explain himself.

Ronald proceeded to tell them that this is our marital home so I cannot deny him entrance. The sergeant asked him to provide documents to prove that the house is his. I concurred and asked him to produce the same. He could say nothing.

I had been in my house for five years before I met him so this man had no hands in the building of my house. Since he could not answer, I explained to the officers that my name is the only one on the land papers for this property as well as the mortgage for my house and that Ronald never hit a nail in my house.

The sergeant proceeded to tell him that he has no claim to my house and cannot force me to give him entrance into my home. Afterwards, I explained to the police officers what had transpired and the reason I believe Ronald made the call.

The sergeant looked at me in awe then took it upon himself to give Ronald some advice. He told Ronald that he should be thankful every day that I allowed him access to my home. He further explained to Ronald that based on all that I told him that any woman would have put him out a long time ago.

All I can say is that God must have sent this gentleman to my home. The words he spoke to Ronald were profound and very timely because he was clearly being advised by someone who was feeding him false information. The sergeant then asked me if I would allow him to go inside to collect his personal items.

I told him that there was no need for that because his items were packed and at the door. I opened the door and the two officers collected his items. The sergeant then escorted Ronald to the police bus and took him away. I could not stop praising God for that deliverance. Satan had left the building!

The following week, I returned to the doctor in New Providence to have the swollen masses checked. I had to have an in-office procedure done to have them drained. God knows that I could take no more pain but it had to be done. Financially, I was exhausted but the bill had to be paid.

After the procedure was done, I healed well and my house returned to normal since Ronald was no longer there. However, he attempted to call and stalk me for a few months afterwards to ensure that I had no other man in my house. I had to be very frank with him and threaten him with the police if he did not stop calling or watching my house. I had no further encounter with him and in December 2014, my children and I moved to New Providence.

Chapter 19: "Reality Check!"

When God gives you instructions you should always obey. I knew better than to disobey a command from God because I had been chastised before but I allowed a man to come into my life and distract me from following what sayeth the Lord. I had been working at the same school for some eight years. While there, I was able to upgrade educationally so I am now Dr. Evans.

While pursuing this degree, I started to feel restless. I knew that I had outgrown the position in which I served but each year I asked God if it was time to move and He always replied, "not yet." That went on for the next four years.

The day finally came when I asked Him the question again and He answered "yes" but I didn't move because my husband wanted to stay. That year I got sick resulting in me having surgery, but after healing from the surgery I had follow-up visits with the doctor for the next twelve months.

I was already financially exhausted and Ronald had left me with the balance on the doctor's bills after agreeing to pay so I had those to pay off as well. To add, Alice was in college and I had household and other responsibilities inclusive of my two younger children so I had to request relocation to New Providence.

God was going to have His way willingly or otherwise. I had forgotten the scripture that said that obedience is better than sacrifice (I Samuel 15:22). I sacrificed a lot as a result of my disobedience. I returned to New Providence broke; I had no money! I had sold just about everything out of my house to finance the move yet I had no money. Honestly, it didn't matter. I was willing to do what I could legally do to move.

While selling items, packing, cleaning, and taking items to the boat for shipping, I felt nothing. I didn't allow myself to feel any sort of emotions or to think about my situation. I was focused and determined to leave not only so that I would be closer to my doctor and less financially burdened but so that I could fix my relationship with my Heavenly Father.

To the carnal mind this was just an unfortunate situation but through my spiritual eyes, this was God's way of getting me where He needed me to be. He told me to leave and I didn't so He forced me to leave and in the process of doing so, He stripped me of all of my fortune; he dried up every stream.

I was doing well on the island where I lived. I have a nice four-bedroom house, my children were always in private school, I drove a nice car that I bought brand new, we ate the best food available, we ate out whenever we wanted, and we had very nice things. We were quite comfortable.

I had my regular job but had several other means of making income which were very lucrative. Life was great for us! Once I disobeyed God, bit my bit things started falling apart until I was stripped down to the bare minimum. I had hit rock bottom in my eyes and I could do nothing about it.

I sent my son ahead of us on the plane while Olivia and I drove to the boat for the four-hour trip to New Providence on the Bo-Hengy fast ferry. Again, I had no emotion. I just did what I knew I had to do and that was to leave that island so I did. Once I arrived in New Providence, Drew was already settled in so Olivia and I took a few days to unpack and get settled.

I found it so strange that my parents nor my siblings said anything to me. I don't know if they just didn't know what to say or they were just respecting my privacy but it was clear that my marriage was over after eight short, miserable months!

Once I had no more unpacking to do or my emotions to guard any longer, reality started to sink in. All of the emotions I had suppressed started to flood me like a tsunami; I was slipping into a depression. I was so numb that I could find no tears to cry. I didn't eat much, I barely slept, and I stayed locked up in my room. All I could do was ponder what had happened and asked God "WHY!"

Again, I felt that I was being punished but I didn't know what I did to deserve this treatment. God knew me and I knew Him so this time was very hard for me because none of what I had gone through or was feeling made any sense. I cried out to God for help but I felt unworthy! That's when the tears started to flow because I didn't know what I had done to upset my Father. God had to be angry at me, otherwise He would have protected me from such pain, humiliation, and financial hardship!

Since God was mad at me, I stopped talking to Him. I was slipping deeper into a depression. The emotional pain of a broken heart was more intense than the pain of the surgery to the point that I just wanted to die. My thinking was that all would be better if God would just put me out of my misery. I could not see my way out of the hole I was in and it was getting deeper by the day.

It was Christmas time but there was nothing joyous or merry about this holiday season for me. Each day from Christmas day, to Boxing Day to those days leading up to New Year's Day I stayed in bed. I don't think my parents knew how to reach me so they didn't try.

I am a trained counselor and I didn't want to be reached. I was having a bigtime pity party for myself until one day I heard the Holy Spirit say softly,

"Get up out of this bed and go outside and just let the breeze hit your face."

That evening was Carnival night for my family. I was feeling so sorry for myself that I had no intention of going but once The Father said to get up I reluctantly did. I don't know what would have happened had I not gotten up but going out and doing what God said changed the course of my life profoundly.

It was a cool evening in late December at The Sports Center grounds where we attended the Christmas Carnival. While out there, the children got themselves in gear to go on all of their favorite rides and those that looked fun.

While standing at the barricade of one of the rides watching Olivia enjoy herself, a series of cool breezes hit my face and I started to come alive again. Let me tell you, it was like God refueled me that night. I was rejuvenated and had mental clarity as to what needed to happen next in my life.

For the next year I struggled financially because I had a lot of past due and current bills. Also, that year I attended counseling sessions because I realized that no matter how good of a counselor I was, I had taken myself as far as I could. I needed help.

Once I spoke with my supervisor, she asked me to select someone I wanted to see so I did what I do best when I have decisions to make; I prayed to Father for guidance. As always, He led me to a wonderful family therapist who I knew and was comfortable with. Overtime, she was able to gradually help me put the pieces of my life back together.

Chapter 20: "Sealing the Deal!"

Getting a divorce was a big decision; one I had to be sure of before I proceeded to have my lawyer file the documents. Once I returned to New Providence, I started the process to seek early release from my marriage. Due to the horrid circumstances, my lawyer was confident that it would be granted.

Since I was the one seeking early release, I had to pay the lawyer bills initially. I was already financially strapped but it had to be done. I needed to be free of this man. For several months I consulted with my attorney, submitted documents, and signed legal papers that needed to be filed with the court to start the process.

While that was going on, I was attending counseling sessions once every week to address my emotional state. I admit that I was an emotional wreck but stable. This was the first time that I was in the client chair. I was always the therapist behind the desk now I was the one who had to pour out my heart and fill out forms regarding my feelings, behaviors, expectations, faults, failures, hurts and the like. The sessions were great but I was asked several tough questions, three of which I will mention.

The first tough question I was asked was "how long did we date?" Wow! I wasn't ready to answer that one because I already knew the answer I was going to get. Once I told her, she responded by saying,

"You should have known better than that. How could you marry someone you have known for less than a year?"

She was right. This man had me convinced that he knew God intimately like I did. He told me that he sang in his church choir and described his conversion on the Airport Road which was similar to Saul's experience on the road to Damascus. He repeated this story during one of the marital counseling sessions which impressed our marriage counselor as well. It was important to me that I married a Christian man so I suppose he decided to become who I needed him to be to win me over. Scary right?

Every week I had a homework assignment. All of it didn't have to do with my marriage. Some of it was personal; pertaining just to me. It was important for her to determine how much this situation had damaged my self-esteem, self-worth, perception of myself, and my view of marriage. Let me just say right here that I felt worthless as a woman because Ronald had no desire to touch me or to be intimate with me. When I touched him, he laughed in my face like I was disgusting.

In reality, this literally made me feel like I was going to have a nervous breakdown! My confidence in my ability to please a man sexually was affected greatly. I didn't know if I could fill that tall order anymore so you know what, I needed to find out whether I still had what it took to excite and please a man so I went on a quest to find out and yes...success; it was not me! The problem was him. I don't encourage any ladies to do what I did but, in my situation, it was necessary for my sanity. (For those of you who are wondering, let me clearly state here that I was fully healed from my surgery and treatments, and disease-free!)

Another hard question I had to answer was: "what did I contribute to our failed marriage" because it could not all be his fault alone right? Well in this case it was all him. However, to be fair, I will tell you what he told me made him not want to be intimate with me then you decide.

Firstly, he told me that I looked down on him because he only had a high school education. As I think about this statement, I can recall numerous occasions when I spoke to him about continuing his education in college and offered my assistance when he was ready.

Secondly, he told me that I talked at him. Ummm. Okay, by asking him to wash dishes or to clean up after himself was that talking down to him? He was very nasty and I kept my house clean. Furthermore, I should not have to tell a grown man to clean up after himself or when to take a bath. I am just saying. Anyway, these are the two reasons he gave as to why he could not get excited in the bedroom. I will leave that right there!

The final question I was asked that I had to ponder upon was "whether I was sure I wanted a divorce." At this point Ronald had started texting me and asking me to forgive him and to give "us" another chance. He must have been desperate because he texted me so much that I didn't answer all of them. I did hear him out though and gave his request some thought. I wanted to ensure that I left no stone unturned when it came to whether my marriage was over or could be saved.

In one of my sessions, my therapist asked me to compare the good and the bad in each relationship of significance that I had been a part of over the years. As superficial as I saw this to be, it was quite helpful because it made me realize that I married Ronald on the rebound because I could not have the man I really wanted at the time.

I had to admit that my role in this failed marriage was that even though I loved Ronald, I was not in love with him; I was in love with the man I went on my emergency 911 quest with. After all was said and done, I told Ronald that there was no turning back. The marriage was over. He was upset but after he got over the shock of my answer, he finally apologized for the way he treated me. A few months later, my request for early dismissal from this marriage was granted.

Even though I am tempted to speak to the ladies only here, I must speak to the men too. A broken heart is a serious thing. It is nothing to play with because if you don't give yourself time to heal, you can make a decision that can devastate your life for a very long time and in some instances an eternity.

Some persons have been scarred so badly by the failure of a past relationship that they never consider marriage again but my brothers and sisters, marriage was ordained by God. I understand that divorce is not something He likes but in my case the risk of death was too great so leaving was the best option for me. Before I made any decision, I prayed to Father and I spoke to my pastor and later got confirmation that leaving was the best option under these circumstances.

When it comes to sexually transmitted diseases, you can't take that lightly. You may be wondering why I would consider staying? Well I loved my husband but I couldn't get past what he did to me.

When I prayed to Father I asked him one specific question. The question was,

"Father please show me how to allow him to touch me and to be intimate with me again without feeling scared and freezing up and I will stay?"

I never got an answer directly. However, when I spoke to my pastor about the same thing he said these profound words to me,

"Sister Evans, I am pro-marriage but I have a wife and sister, and if any of them came to me with a situation like yours, in good conscience, I couldn't ask them to stay."

That was a moment to cry tears of joy right there but I could find none to cry. All I did was thank him and hung up the phone. I had gotten my answer. After Ronald had painted a picture of me being the one sleeping around in our marriage the truth was finally revealed. "Oh, what a tangled web we weave…" You know the rest.

Chapter 21: "To Date or Not to Date"

There are so many people who have negative perceptions about counseling, in fact to many it is still a bit taboo. As a counselor myself, I can tell you that I needed help after my marriage fell apart and I was not ashamed to admit it.

However, there are persons suffering through many of life's difficulties and they are silently falling apart just to save face amongst those they love or value as important to them. No one wants to be viewed as crazy so they suffer in silence. This thinking is very unwise and can prove detrimental to your mental stability if not changed.

The course of my life started to change over the course of my counseling and more so after the six months ended. I was happy. I got my joy back and for the first time in a long time, I felt encouraged that my life was not over and that I would love again. Once my sessions ended, I had to face the reality of life alone. What was I going to do? I had not thought about it. I didn't know what I wanted to do. My divorce process was just starting so I had a long road ahead.

I can remember when I was asked out on a date (by a man) for the first time after my separation. I didn't know how to think about that. It had been almost a year since I had returned to New Providence but I had no desire to go out with anyone to do anything. I spent my time reconnecting with me and enjoying the company of my children. Life was great for me so going out on a date was not even a thought, therefore, nowhere in my plans.

I was so not accustomed to the new dating scene that I sought advice from a female friend. She was very candid in her advice which I appreciated. She told me not to rush going out until I felt ready to do so. I took her advice and before I went out with anyone, I got to know them a bit first.

The first guy who spoke to me was a parent and he seemed nice so I took a risk and went out with him. We went to dinner at a popular eatery. The food was great but all he did was talk about himself all night.

"Is this what dating today is like?" I thought.
It was like he was selling a pitch and he hoped I was buying. I was not impressed. In fact, his approach was scary and I didn't need scary considering all I had been through.

After the date, this man called and texted me every day and even proposed marriage. He even sent me pictures of engagement rings!

"No....No! I can't do this. What is this man thinking?" I pondered. "All of this after one date! Are the pickings that slim?" I wondered.

After sharing my concerns with my female friend, I learned that many women were as wild and loose as the men; hence, not too in a hurry to settle down or commit. Now it made sense why this man was so enchanted. As for me…. I ran away from him as fast as I could, blocked and deleted him. However, he had another phone and continued his attempt to woo me against my will. He had become a stalker. To get rid of him, I had to change my phone number all together. That experience scared me so much that I didn't consider dating for another year. I learned to be content.

I had my share of dating here and there but nothing that stood out to me. I was not really too eager to get involved in anything too deep until I was divorced but at the same time, I wanted to feel desired and needed.

I remember this brief relationship I had. This man was a year my senior so I decided to give him a try. Let me tell you something, there are many crazy men on these streets people and many of them believe that their craziness is the new normal! He was a serious kind of crazy. He believed that any woman who had a problem with him smoking weed was crazy.

He had a skewed perception of the world and what was going on in it. He is one of those men who has no problem letting a woman take care of him. We have a name for men like that don't we ladies? He is a gigolo! Finally, all of his views were antichrist, immoral, very argumentative, just negative, and get this; he did not sleep. Just freaky!

Ladies, let me tell you my heart. We get desperate. We get hard up and we feel as if we are on some time line to enjoy our lives and snag a man but if I can be real, that's when we make bad decisions and mess up! What is so sad is that we all see the signs and notice their flaws, yet we indulge them. We know that we can't introduce these jokers to anyone but because we are lonely we entertain these stupid men. Stop it!

You need to know your worth and not settle for the first man who winks at you or tells you that you are gorgeous. You need to learn to consult Father before you spend your precious time with any man. God told us in Jeremiah 29: 11-

"For I know the plans I have for you," declares the Lord, "plans to prosper you and not harm you, plans to give you hope and a future."

You need to realize that you are the gem; you are the prize not him. If a man can't see your worth mama move on. You don't owe him any apology or explanation. All he needs to hear is,

"Sorry love, this is not working for me."

The end!

too in a hurry to settle down or commit. Now it made sense why this man was so enchanted. As for me…. I ran away from him as fast as I could, blocked and deleted him. However, he had another phone and continued his attempt to woo me against my will. He had become a stalker. To get rid of him, I had to change my phone number all together. That experience scared me so much that I didn't consider dating for another year. I learned to be content.

I had my share of dating here and there but nothing that stood out to me. I was not really too eager to get involved in anything too deep until I was divorced but at the same time, I wanted to feel desired and needed.

I remember this brief relationship I had. This man was a year my senior so I decided to give him a try. Let me tell you something, there are many crazy men on these streets people and many of them believe that their craziness is the new normal! He was a serious kind of crazy. He believed that any woman who had a problem with him smoking weed was crazy.

He had a skewed perception of the world and what was going on in it. He is one of those men who has no problem letting a woman take care of him. We have a name for men like that don't we ladies? He is a gigolo! Finally, all of his views were antichrist, immoral, very argumentative, just negative, and get this; he did not sleep. Just freaky!

Ladies, let me tell you my heart. We get desperate. We get hard up and we feel as if we are on some time line to enjoy our lives and snag a man but if I can be real, that's when we make bad decisions and mess up! What is so sad is that we all see the signs and notice their flaws, yet we indulge them. We know that we can't introduce these jokers to anyone but because we are lonely we entertain these stupid men. Stop it!

You need to know your worth and not settle for the first man who winks at you or tells you that you are gorgeous. You need to learn to consult Father before you spend your precious time with any man. God told us in Jeremiah 29: 11-

"For I know the plans I have for you," declares the Lord, "plans to prosper you and not harm you, plans to give you hope and a future."

You need to realize that you are the gem; you are the prize not him. If a man can't see your worth mama move on. You don't owe him any apology or explanation. All he needs to hear is,

"Sorry love, this is not working for me."

The end!

SECTION 6
The Original Doorway: Coming Full Circle

Chapter 22: "Please Don't Touch Me There"

Being back home was going great. In fact, I had resumed all of the things I loved doing like lecturing and counseling. I even opened a business at the advice of a colleague who saw a need for my services to be offered privately.

Once I opened, God blessed my business and it continued to evolve until it became what He envisioned it to become. I didn't question any of it. I just fell in line with whatever God instructed. Today I have a full-fledged learning, counseling, and career center.

I became a part of a support group at work under the umbrella of "The Family" that was established for counselors during the week to share and offload stresses of our profession. This was a very good initiative because the question had always been asked;

"Who counsels the ones who counsels them all?"

The answer to that question had always been,

"No one."

So this group was established; the innovative and timely vision of Dr. David Allen, a well-known medical doctor and psychologist in The Bahamas. This group opened the door for me to attend Saturday morning training sessions with this man who is a pioneer in his field and a well-respected author. His team is wonderful as well.

After attending and participating in the weekend sessions with the group for some months, I was asked a few times by Dr. Allen to speak about my experience with domestic violence and give insight into the false self which I had no problem discussing since I had become comfortable with the group. I was even on his television show to speak about my experience. These sessions opened the door for me to talk about that horrific experience but also to help persons heal from their own horrible experiences.

When I decided to attend these sessions, I had no idea what was going to happen, because I only went to learn under the tutelage of this accomplished expert in his field. However, little did I know, God had plans to bust the door of my past wide open and expose my original doorway!

During one of the Saturday sessions the topic discussed was sexual abuse and its prevalence today versus the past. Many persons spoke about how in the past this type of abuse was accepted in many communities and not spoken about when it was uncovered, resulting in many children suffering in silence.

Others stated that even though more of it is reported today, they still believe sexual abuse is happening more than is being reported. I sat there and listened because I really could say nothing. I felt so personally drawn to the topic but didn't really know why.

As persons spoke, I started to have flashes of memory of me in a room with a man. The visions were not clear but I saw enough to remember that I was abused at the hand of my paternal grandfather at a young age. What was so profound was that I had recently had the dream of me in the dark room and falling from a high building as described at the beginning of this book.

As my memories unraveled in this room, I didn't know how to feel. I was terrified and anxious at the same time. Suddenly my life started to make sense. My fascination with studies on incest resulting in me conducting my own study on incest as I worked on my first degree. My fear of intimacy and anything sexual, and my inability to engage in sexual activity until I was a young adult.

My bullying of children who were vulnerable and weak in any setting I saw them in (including church) was one of the ways I lashed out. In fact, church was my favorite place to pinch and hit little girls. I was hurt so I inflicted pain on children especially females. I even wrote love letters to boys and engaged in a little hanky panky with the boy next door.

"My lord, what kind of mischief was this?" I wondered.

Once we broke off into small groups and the discussion become more intimate, I was one of the persons who spoke about my experience. I did not go into great details in the group but I got an opportunity to role play which was great. Let me not get ahead of myself. I will start at the beginning. Here is what happened when I was a child.

I was about eight years old. I lived on a multi-family lot with my parents in one house and my grandparents in another. My parents were poor but they provided for us the best way they could. My father was the only parent in my house who worked outside the home. My mommy was a housewife; which means that she stayed home and took care of the house and us. There were four children in the family at the time.

My father was very strict. He didn't allow us to stay after school to play or play in the neighborhood with other children. Instead, we played in our yard or in our house. However, there was one place I looked forward to going to after school though, and that was to visit my Grammy Lucy who lived in the house right in front of ours.

She was a janitress at one of the local high schools in town. I loved spending time with her because she gave me lots of treats and sent me to run errands to buy items at the grocery store or to deliver packages to her cousin who lived up the street from us. My memories of times spent at her house had always been great until that day when something traumatic happened that changed my life forever!

Grammy Lucy was married to my paternal grandfather Roy which made her my step-grandmother but you would never know that because she treated all of us like her very own blood grandchildren. Grandpa Roy was a fisherman by trade and an alcoholic the rest of the time. I can't remember him being sober for one day! However, he didn't mistreat my Grammy but something must have been wrong between them because they slept in separate bedrooms. To add, Grandpa Roy was very scary to be around!

One afternoon, I was visiting my Grammy Lucy and Grandpa Roy called me from his back bedroom. His bedroom was the dark scary room right past the kitchen. He never opened the windows or the curtains, nor turned on the light so this day was no different. This made the room dusty and stuffy with a musty smell. I was surprised that he was at home because he was usually out until late into the night getting drunk.

He called for me again so I went. As I walked towards the room, I was afraid and nervous at the same time.

"What could Grandpa Roy be calling me for?" I wondered.

"His wife was right in her room so shouldn't he be calling her?" I pondered

When I got to the room, the door was closed so I pushed it open. He turned, looked at me then motioned with his hand for me to come closer to the bed where he laid so I did. Once I got to the side of the bed, I realized that he was drunk. Before, I realized it, the unthinkable happened! Grandpa Roy had put his hand under my dress and began to touch me.

He then pulled my panties down. I froze with fear. I could not move. He then began to unbuckle his pants. I just stood there staring. After he zipped down his pants, he lifted me on top of him. I do not know how much time had passed before Grammy Lucy pushed the door open. Once she did, I jumped off the bed as fast as I could and ran home. I was so afraid I never told my parents what happened.

I do not know what Grammy Lucy saw, what she thought happened, or what she thought of me from that day onward. I can tell you that she never spoke to me about what happened. She never told my parents either. Instead, I suffered in silence every day, filled with confusion, fear, guilt and shame. My life was never the same again!

What a horrible experience for a young child to go through right? All I can say is that God allowed me to repress those memories for many years, until at the age of eighteen, when I started to have those dreams of being in that house but I was still unable to put the pieces of the puzzle together until many years later.

For years I was afraid of that house and didn't like to go into that kitchen. I cannot recall ever going back into that house while Grandpa Roy was there. I always felt different though. I don't know why but I got this label of *black sheep* branded to me which I recently broke off my life.

When my grandfather died, I remember seeing him in our house after the funeral. I was petrified! When I walked into the house pass the dining room table, there he was standing in my parents' bedroom doorway. I knew it was his spirit but that didn't make it less scary and I was a child so fear took over.

That night my mother must have seen him too because she was in that room with her olive oil rebuking and casting out and damning something to hell! I never saw him again, but it was clear that his spirit never left that property.

Chapter 23: "Elementary School Days – Acting Out and Becoming a Bully"

After months of confusion, I had to decide to not let my negative encounter with Grandpa Roy affect my life, but it did. I was in fourth grade and I can remember being a bully. I found the most timid and vulnerable child to pick on and tease. I took children's lunch money and would hit (or pinch) them for no reason.

My behavior was so bizarre that I acted the same way in church. I would sit next to the little girl who was alone and pinch her just to make her cry then leave. I was hostile towards other children and I could not understand the reason for my behavior. What was scary about this is that I enjoyed it!

Besides this, I had no interest in school so my grades were always very bad. I made mostly D's, E's, and F's; maybe the occasional B or C. In spite of these grades, I was a very smart student but no one would ever know this because my bad behavior overshadowed my smarts.

I refused to study, I barely did any homework, and I didn't pay attention in class. I was more concerned with eating lunch, playing, and beating up children. I was on the path to destruction. My parents didn't realize how bad my behavior was because I didn't act this way at home. In fact, I was a saint in their presence.

I can remember my behavior getting so bad that at the end of Grade 4, I was expelled from the private school I attended. The principal told my mother that I was no longer welcomed in that school. This was the year that my education in the public-school system began. I can honestly say that I showed concern for my education for the first time in my young life because until that moment, I had only known private school education. A new chapter of my life was about to begin.

I started Grade five in a new environment and for the first time, my behavior was tamed. In reality, I had no choice because I didn't know what to expect from this new school. I was placed in the lowest stream with all of the children with behavioral problems and low grades; like me.

That year I performed extremely well, making the principal's list, and that trend continued through Grade 6 when I was placed in the top stream. I made some great friends in that new school. I truly enjoyed my two years there.

Even though my behavior had improved at school, I became more mischievous at home. My mind was not on playing regular little girl games such as doll house or fixing hair; in fact, I was more interested in playing with boys. There was a boy who lived across the street who took a liking to me and me to him. He and I played our own version of "mommy and daddy" which was not a game a child should have been playing.

You see, since I had been exposed to sex from my grandfather, I developed an interest in continuing to explore this new-found venture. Therefore, Munroe and I got very "touchy feely." I can't say all of the things we did, but it involved inappropriate touching. I can even remember a time when I took the grass out of the yard and tried to smoke it. Was I going crazy? I don't think so.

However, I was trying to find ways to get the attention I needed from my parents who had no clue what had happened to me or what I was engaging in right under their noses. My behavior was a cry for help, but no one heard me! I continued to suffer alone.

Chapter 24: "Pre-teen Years – My First Taste of Love"

After doing all of those bizarre things to hurt myself and others, one day I just stopped. I was getting older and had developed an infatuation with the boy next door. Nathan was a handsome boy around the same age as me. He actually had a liking for me too. We started writing each other love letters and he became my focus. This went on for months.

In fact, in my mind we were secretly boyfriend and girlfriend. I found myself going outside just to get a glimpse of him as he passed their kitchen window. I would play on the side of my grandmother's house just so he could see me. This angered Munroe who thought that he was my boyfriend. However, he and I remained friends but we didn't play together anymore.

I had gotten so attached to Nathan through my letters that I would dare say that I was in love; puppy love I suppose. Our secret relationship was the highlight of my life at eleven years old until one day we were exposed. One of the letters I had written to Nathan was found by his brothers who threatened to tell both our parents about our relationship if we didn't end it.

Need-less-to-say, whatever relationship I thought we had was now over. From that point on, I was taunted by those brothers and made to feel as if I had committed the greatest sin in the world by falling in love.

While in grade seven, I started to become wild in school again. I loved playing games during the lunch and break times and would always arrive to class late. I had my little clique that I ran and lead them in bad behavior as well. We did our school work but I was a negative influence on them as far as work ethics was concerned.

It was in this grade that I found out that I had problems with vision and started wearing glasses. Well, wearing glasses was not fashionable back then so as you may have guessed, I got teased.

At first it bothered me and I didn't wear them, but when my Spanish teacher threatened me by stating that I could not come back to her class without them, that's when I started to wear them more often.

At that point it really didn't matter to me what the students thought because I needed my glasses to see the blackboard so that I could learn. That year I did better in school. However, I was still not working at my fullest potential.

In grade eight, I continued to do well in school, but I remained playful. This year was when my life changed for the better. It was at the end of this year that I was nominated to become a school prefect. Remember me saying that I led students to do bad things? Subsequently, one of the teachers saw that and recommended me to become a school prefect. I suppose her rationale was that if I could lead students to do bad things then I could lead them to do good things.

    Well folks, she was right. I became a school prefect in grade nine and I took that post extremely serious! I became a school police and I can say with assurance that no one could break any school rules on my watch. I manned my posts with sternness and much pride!

Chapter 25: "Withdrawn and Depressed"

After my relationship with Nathan ended, I became depressed because I didn't understand why we could no longer speak. Shortly after that, his family moved away which made matters worse. I started to become more playful in school again. However, I made sure that I maintained the minimum grade point average.

I started having these strange feelings like I was being haunted. I would have weird dreams and wake up scared to death but I could not remember the dreams. Grandpa Roy had died while I was still in primary school, which had no emotional impact on me at all. I didn't feel anything.

In fact, there was a part of me that was happy, because I was afraid of him. Could this be him haunting me? I had no answers. Besides the strange dreams, I would wake up from my sleep and could not move. I felt paralyzed or like someone was restricting me from moving. At this time in my life, I started to pray more and it was only when I prayed that the force that held me down would release me. What was happening to me?

Additionally, when Grandpa Roy died, a part of me died with him. It is hard to explain the emotional disconnection I had because I was a child, but something else happened. Grandpa Roy was a fisherman. He would bring home all of the fish, conch, crawfish, and lobster and all sea creatures imaginable which we thoroughly enjoyed. He would bring home crab too!

Once he died, I developed an allergy to all of these foods except fish. In fact, whenever my mother would cook any of them, I had to leave the house because the smell of them made me sick to my stomach. There again, I didn't make the connection between what I was currently experiencing and what had previously happened to me at the hand of Grandpa Roy.

I became a Christian in Grade nine, but I was around nine years old when I first started praying to God and I knew that He heard my prayers and would help me with my confusion. I would cuddle up between the refrigerator and the stove in the kitchen to pray and sing to the Lord. I would pray for three things: wisdom, knowledge and understanding. I would also sing songs I heard on the radio and those that I loved such as "Whisper a Prayer in the Morning."

As I continued to pray, I also prayed for a spirit of discernment and insight. I can honestly say that God hears the prayers of children and those of the faithful because he granted me each of these things I prayed for. That year, I sat eleven BJC's and passed all of them with "C" grades and better.

In grade ten, I became head girl. Wow, what a great accomplishment for a girl who started off so playful, rude, and unconcerned about her education! This new post consumed my life so much that I didn't have any time to feel depressed, think about the weird dreams I was having, or being haunted. I took this responsibility very seriously which meant that many things in my life had to change.

I took my education more seriously, dove into my books and became the top of my class. I wanted to do well in school (and in life) so I researched what I needed to do to become successful. I knew that my parents could not afford to pay for me to go to college so I needed to know all of the scholarships that were available at that time. I had a plan for my life for the first time and felt that college was in my future.

That year was a very interesting one because I started to notice that there were some girls who had not returned to school. Some were from my grade level while others were from a grade level lower. My classmates and I never spoke about it, but I was able to put the pieces of the puzzle together and realized that those girls were no longer with us because they got pregnant.

With that new-found knowledge, I became withdrawn and swore off boys and relationships. I was not about to get pregnant so boyfriends were out of the question for me! That became my rule: No boyfriends!

Ok, yes there were guys that I liked and yes, I had guy friends, but I guess I was so naïve that I didn't realize that they liked me when they did. Even though I had not figured out that I was molested as yet, I suppose deep down inside I felt dirty, used, cheap, and ashamed. The thought of anything intimate or sexual, no matter how innocent or mild terrified me. I had developed a fear of males. I felt as if all they wanted to do was hurt me, use me and abuse me. No, no, I was not about to allow that to happen! I became the watchman over my body and my heart.

Chapter 26: "Teen years – Rebellion of the Black Sheep"

Somehow, I became the black sheep of my family. I never understood why I was called that name but I was. I found myself fighting for mere privileges that my older sister got so I rebelled. When my father told me that I had to be home right after school, if I had something to do or somewhere to go I did that before I came home.

I was not a promiscuous teen, no, quite the opposite. I was very much into my books and doing well in school. I had joined Junior Achievement, The Police Cadet Corp Program and numerous clubs at school, which kept me very busy. Juggling all of these activities still left room for me to maintain honor roll status and become head girl once again in grade 12.

Even though I was more focused in school, I was a mess internally. I never felt whole. I felt lonely a lot and was hard on myself. I always felt that I could do better than I was doing. I was not a people's person. In fact, I was very quiet and reserved (Those who know me now may find that hard to believe).

Don't get me wrong, I spoke when the opportunity presented itself, but I never volunteered to speak to anyone. I was very self-conscious of my image and maintained a very petite physique. I was athletic and was a part of the track team. I had all of these great dreams to one day make it to the Olympics, but I talked myself out of pursuing that dream, telling myself that I was not good enough; that I would never make it!

All of the negative self-talk I had with myself made me a very angry teen. I cried myself to sleep most nights because I was grossly lonely and unhappy. I was needy so I wanted to be loved by my parents in a way they didn't give. I know they loved us and wanted the best for us, but I didn't get love in the way I needed it.

Let me be clear, my parents provided greatly for us and they pushed us to do well, but hearing the words "I love you," or getting a hug was what I needed most of all. I needed positive affirmations from my parents which I didn't get. I became an unpleasant youth.

Listen, I had old school parents. They grew up hard. They didn't hear the words "I love you" from their parents so I understood the reason they couldn't say that to us. My father told us his story of hardship and moving around from one house to the next while growing up. He was not raised by his mother or father but many surrogate parents who became his family.

He knew his parents but he just didn't live with them. His parents were unmarried so that came along with its own dynamics. Consequently, my father learned to hustle and work hard to survive so that became his focus as a young boy and remained his focus as an adult man.

I remember the day my father and I had a falling out. I was at home watching television and when he came home he turned it off to listen to his records. There was only one television in the house and it was in the living room. My father also had his record player in the living room which he played every evening when he came home.

Well, that particular evening, I was not going to have him bully me so I turned the television back on. I told him that I was watching that, but it didn't matter so he clicked it back off and I clicked it back on. That clicking the television off and on went on for a minute until he slapped me.

That was it for me. I stormed out of the house and walked to my girlfriend's house who lived about 20 minutes away. When I got there, I told her what had happened. I told her that I was moving out, and that I couldn't take his attitude anymore. That was the start of the rocky relationship with my father.

It was around midnight when my mother called and told me that it was safe to come back home. She told me that she had spoken to my father and told him that if he hit me again that she would call the police. I went back home, but my father didn't talk to me for more than two months. It was like walking on eggshells in our house, but one thing I learned that night and that was that my mother loved me and had my back. I know that my father loved me too, but his iron-fist method of running his house was not working for me.

My parents had raised us well, but I felt that they didn't have much faith in what they had instilled in us. Some parents do not realize that their children have feelings too and should be respected. All my father had to do was ask me to turn the television off so that he could listen to his records or just allow me to finish watching my program then play his records.

Growing up in a house with my parents was not easy. They were too strict. I felt like I had to fight for opportunities that they could have easily helped me obtain and accomplish. I felt like I was doing everything alone. That was a horrible feeling as a teenager of fifteen years old.

Chapter 27: "Senior Year – My First True Love"

At the end of grade 12, I had my first real boyfriend and it was great. Two-months shy of graduation I started dating this young man who impacted my life profoundly. Allen was a year my senior and we had known each other for about nine months. He was tall, dark, and so handsome with smooth complexion, but I was afraid to let him touch me. I had developed a phobia for sex and intimacy. At sixteen years old, I had fallen in love and it felt wonderful! He was a true gentleman.

At the time he and I started dating, I was well on my way preparing for prom. He was not my prom date, because I had already been asked to the prom, but I was his date to a very important work banquet several months later which was fabulous. We looked so good together that I thought that we would be a couple forever. For the first time in my life, I felt worthy of love and allowed myself to be loved by him. I gave myself permission to love him.

He and I were inseparable. I was now a student at The College of the Bahamas and he was working with a government agency. What I loved about him was that he never pushed or forced me to do anything. He did not understand the reason for my phobia and neither did I at the time so all I would say to him was that I was not ready. That was always enough for him. We enjoyed each other's company in very innocent yet fun ways such as going out to eat, hanging out by his house or going for drives. We were young so fun for us was easy.

My parents were not liking the fact that we were dating. They were against us girls having boyfriends. Even though I respected my parents, this time I was not ending my relationship. I introduced Allen to my parents so they knew who he was, but they still did not approve of the relationship.

They could not give me a reason though, which bothered me because if they were so against me seeing him then at least they should tell me why. Well, I later learned that it did not have anything to do with him, per se. They would have felt the same way about any guy. Our relationship continued to flourish and I became very close with his family.

Our relationship was great for the year it lasted, and when it ended, the rollercoaster of emotions started again. I felt like it was my fault that he had chosen someone else over me. This defeat gave me permission to beat myself up again which I continued to do for many years thereafter. We eventually got back together a few years later but I believe that we had many forces working against us.

Firstly, we found out that his grandmother was my mother's fourth or fifth cousin which was a no-no for us dating and secondly, I had gotten involved in another relationship while we were apart which he never forgave me for. Even though he had moved on as well, he still had this notion that I was his. Go figure!

Section 7
Complete Deliverance: The Final Fight for My Freedom through the Blood of Christ Jesus

Chapter 28: "The Jezebel Spirit"

I feel like I have been fighting all of my life but once I discovered why I was fighting; I felt pretty good. I could finally breathe a sigh of relief and begin to live my life now. I was happily single and loving my life reconnecting with The Lord. I was not having any challenges or fights. Life was good. I finally got to the point where I was ready to begin writing this book. I can honestly say that I had good and bad days as I wrote. I got so overwhelmed at times that I asked God if He was sure that I needed to be writing this book. He told me "yes". However, whenever I got overwhelmed I stopped until I felt ready to resume.

I remember this one particular time when I stopped for about a month. The pain I felt was so overwhelming that I could not proceed. I sent my manuscript for my friend Ruth to read and she did. This was not the first time I had sent her my work to read but this time was different. You see my friend has the gift of prophesy which means that she can see in the spirit realm. I know that some of you don't believe in that or cannot even relate to what I am saying but regardless of whether you believe in it or not; it exists.

One day she contacted me and told me that she was concerned about what she was seeing. Of course, I got concerned as well because I know that her gift is real since I had experienced it before. However, this time she told me that I had a strong dark spirit hovering over my life. She identified it as a Jezebel spirit. I had no idea what this spirit was and what it was doing in my life.

She did tell me that this spirit was the reason for my many failed relationships. She further explained that the spirit entered my life through a sexual doorway. I was distraught because I thought that I had fought off all the spirits operating in my life through fasting and praying. Well, I was so wrong. This fight would turn out to be my biggest one ever because this time it was personal. This spirit was after me not only to make me miserable, but to prevent me from fulfilling my purpose.

As she explained to me the ways this spirit was manipulating things in my life unbeknownst to me, I really didn't know what to say. I was so tired of fighting...honestly, but I knew that if I did nothing, I was going to have a lonely unhappy existence and that is not the type of life Christ wants for His children.

Once I got over the shock of this news, I decided to fight! I started to learn about this spirit so that I would know what it is. Once I did, I understood how dangerous this spirit really is. I spent the next few days listening to teachings on this Jezebel spirit. One thing was for certain, I could not fight it on my own so I told Ruth that I would speak with my pastor.

I went to see him the following week but the days leading up to me going to see him, God showed me what was to come and without fail when I went to see him, he told me exactly what the Lord allowed me to see days prior. He told me that he will turn my case over to a few ladies from the church whose prayer life would be at the level needed to handle such a session. I laughed and told him that I knew that he was going to do that.

Furthermore, he told me that he is familiar with that spirit and that it would be dealt with and had to be broken off of my life. I had no idea what to expect from this meeting with the ladies. I did not know what to call what we were going to be doing but one thing I knew for sure and that was that I needed to dress comfortably and carry my Bible; which I did.

The day of the meeting came which was exactly two days later on a Friday. I was nervous. I knew that once we were done with this session that my life was not going to be the same. Ruth told me not to worry, that I would be fine but from the time she told me about that spirit and exposed it, I had strange things happening. I had something pinch my left upper arm, bite me on my leg while in my bed (under the blanket), and call my name in the voice of my eight-year-old. I couldn't see anything but I was quite aware that the spirit was angry.

Regardless of that, this meeting was going to take place. I arrived at our church office fifteen minutes early. I didn't want any delays in this process beginning. Once the ladies got there, we went into Sister Elizabeth's office. We were alone in the building so God was able to have his way and He surely did.

Chapter 29: "Discovering and Breaking the Generational Curse"

The ladies leading the session are powerful prayer warriors so I had no doubt that I was going to have this Jezebel spirit broken off of my life that night. I was ready. We began with a word of prayer then I was asked to explain what was happening. I revealed to them what I was told about the Jezebel spirit operating in my life and that I needed it removed.

I told them when I believe it entered my life and how it was able to strengthen. As I spoke, Sister Mary wrote down words. She told me that it was important for her to not forget anything that I said and assured me that the paper would be destroyed at the conclusion of the session. I relayed all of the challenges, trials, fights and pitfalls that I had experienced in my life as an adult.

When I was done Sister Mary stated that as she was coming to the session that God told her to ask me a few specific things. Firstly, she asked me about my relationship with my parents and grandparents so I answered. Secondly, she asked me about my grandmothers specifically my paternal grandmother and her husband.

I was shocked because in my mind I had this thing figured out. There was no way this spirit entered my life as a child, right? I thought it but didn't want to believe it because I didn't have sex as a child. I was molested. Once I explained what happened in my grandparents' house, Sister Mary started drawing bricks like a foundation of a building then she added more bricks upon them until she had a building. On several bricks in each row she wrote words from the list she had made as I spoke.

By the time she was done, she explained that what I was battling was deeper than I could imagine. She told me that I was battling a generational curse that started generations before mine and my grandfather's.

To state it in clearer terms, Sister Mary believes that this type of sexual behavior did not start with my grandfather but generations prior. It went down so deep in our family line that she could not say how far back.

However, she stated that the foundation was laid in my life at around eight-years-old with the first encounter with a man – my grandfather – and since then, my life was inculcated with negative contacts of the sexual nature and all of its associates of hurt, manipulation, intimidation, anger, adultery, hatred, unforgiveness, low self-esteem, and the like. All resulting in a sexless marriage.

I was stunned yet relieved because I now knew that my original doorway was the reason for all of this unleashing of negative (and in some instances vile) spirits and principalities into my life.

Once we knew what spirits we were fighting, the deliverance session began. I was told that because these spirits were operating in my life for so long that my deliverance would take time. I had to be prepared to go through the process for as long as it took. We had to now tear down, pluck up, pull down and denounce every evil spirit and principality that had attached itself to my life for the past thirty-six years or more.

I will not go into full detail as to what transpired but I can say this; once the praying and interceding began, I never screamed and cried so much in all my life. I felt pain and hurt that were buried so deep within me rising up and being released.

It is so important that you surrender all to the Lord if you want to be delivered. Once I did, it opened the door for Him to operate in my life and evict every vile spirit and principality that had been operating legally (yes legally) in my life for decades. I never asked to be molested but I was. That one act provided a doorway to Satan and as you read, my life became volatile since then until God took a hold of me and started a work in me.

As Sister Mary and Sister Elizabeth prayed, cast down, and anointed me with Olive Oil, God revealed other ailments to Sister Mary that had been plaguing me as well because she started to experience a very bad headache and the twitching of her left eye;

ailments I had been battling. Well, it didn't take long for that spirit to detach itself from me.

Sister Mary and Sister Elizabeth were working hard but the work was not only that of the ladies. Sister Elizabeth told me that I had to call those people by name who were involved in the building of this fortress (or contributed to it in some way) that had been holding me bond for years. I had to say what they did to me, forgive them and release them to God.

Let me tell you something, the pain and hurt that I released in screams for the second time, I had never heard from my mouth before. In fact, they didn't come from my mouth, they came from that deep dark place where I had hidden all of my hurt and where I assume those spirits enjoyed spending time laughing and jeering at me.

As I released the screams, spoke the names of those persons involved, and the tears fell, I felt a cleansing from within. Sister Elizabeth told me that I will hold my head down in shame no more. She took my chin and lifted my head up as I wept uncontrollably.

Once we were done, the ladies spoke to me and told me that I could not afford to re-open any of the doors that were closed tonight. It was clear that since the original door was opened with illegal sexual contact, that I could no longer allow myself to fall into any such sex trap again.

I had to be prepared to live my life holy and acceptable before the Lord. What was so profound about what they said was that God had already told me that and I disobeyed Him. I was not about to make that mistake again. That night, I had a spiritual awakening like no other. I realized that I had to walk a different walk than many others because of the call on my life and if I didn't, the price I would pay would be great!

This session lasted three hours and afterwards, I felt different. I felt so free. I felt no shame; no blame, just peace and forgiveness. I was ready to begin my new life not only as a redeemed woman of God but a completely delivered woman of God. However, I had no idea what I would experience that night once I got home.

Chapter 30: "Tormented and Intimidated by Evil"

I had been in warfare before but never had I experienced anything like what I experienced the night of my deliverance session. I had been freed of spirits that had me bound for thirty-six years and I had no knowledge of their presence in my life. They had gotten so comfortable that while I was battling other spirits, they were not even moved. Now that they had been evicted, they decided to not only visit me but make my life miserable the entire night.

I didn't experience anything right away when I got home. In fact, I was so happy! I went about my nightly routine as usual then I went to bed. Once I hit my bed it started. I didn't know what I was feeling at first until I had to remind myself of what God's presence feels like then I realized that what I was feeling had to be evil.

Something surrounded me in my bed like a swarm of bees and covered the edge of my bed. No matter which way I turned it was there. The way I felt, this had to be more than one spirit but I didn't know for sure.

I felt like this entity was trying to suffocate me. It could not enter me but it was surely working hard to scare me and it was working until I started to pray. I didn't know what else to do so I did what I knew to do; call on the name of the Lord, Jesus Christ.

I had to be prepared to live my life holy and acceptable before the Lord. What was so profound about what they said was that God had already told me that and I disobeyed Him. I was not about to make that mistake again. That night, I had a spiritual awakening like no other. I realized that I had to walk a different walk than many others because of the call on my life and if I didn't, the price I would pay would be great!

This session lasted three hours and afterwards, I felt different. I felt so free. I felt no shame; no blame, just peace and forgiveness. I was ready to begin my new life not only as a redeemed woman of God but a completely delivered woman of God. However, I had no idea what I would experience that night once I got home.

Chapter 30: "Tormented and Intimidated by Evil"

I had been in warfare before but never had I experienced anything like what I experienced the night of my deliverance session. I had been freed of spirits that had me bound for thirty-six years and I had no knowledge of their presence in my life. They had gotten so comfortable that while I was battling other spirits, they were not even moved. Now that they had been evicted, they decided to not only visit me but make my life miserable the entire night.

I didn't experience anything right away when I got home. In fact, I was so happy! I went about my nightly routine as usual then I went to bed. Once I hit my bed it started. I didn't know what I was feeling at first until I had to remind myself of what God's presence feels like then I realized that what I was feeling had to be evil.

Something surrounded me in my bed like a swarm of bees and covered the edge of my bed. No matter which way I turned it was there. The way I felt, this had to be more than one spirit but I didn't know for sure.

I felt like this entity was trying to suffocate me. It could not enter me but it was surely working hard to scare me and it was working until I started to pray. I didn't know what else to do so I did what I knew to do; call on the name of the Lord, Jesus Christ.

He told me what to do. I got my Bible out and I read it and I played my praise and worship music. I thought that what I did was enough but it wasn't. That darkness was not moved. It surrounded me and it made sure I knew it was there.

I prayed in my spirit and cried out to God for help. I asked Him what to do - do I play music? He told me that I could do that but He wanted me to find a teaching on the Spiritual Gift of Knowledge so I did. However, before I did, I saturated the atmosphere with praise and worship music.

I am big on praise and worship so I got in God's presence and I made up my mind that if I had to contend with this darkness all night that I was going to let God minister to me all night. This evil presence was not about to win!

I found the teaching and turned it on. As I listened to it, I forgot all about that evil that surrounded me and fell asleep. When I woke up through the night, the teaching had ended and the dark presence was gone. I went back to sleep.

The next morning, I messaged Sister Elizabeth and told her what had happened that night. She told me that she should have warned me that the spirits would try to return and surely, they did. She spoke to me about some things to do such as cleansing my space, removing any objects from my space that could attract negative energy or that Satan could use as a doorway and praying and asking God to reveal to me any unrequited sins; all of which I did. In fact, as I prayed the latter, God showed me other persons I needed to call by name, forgive, and release to Him.

Later that morning, Sister Mary called and we spent hours on the telephone talking about what I could expect for the road ahead. I was slowly beginning to realize more and more why Satan was fighting me so hard for so many years. Yes, I had been violated at an early age, but Satan had a plan to use this doorway to destroy me so that my purpose in Christ would not be fulfilled.

Since that didn't work, he found other doorways in my life to bind me up. Hence, my struggles with insecurity, self-esteem, self-doubt, anger, and depression. It was an internal fight to keep myself "fixed" to do well throughout school. I felt like I was always fighting myself and honestly, I was.

I had an opportunity after Sister Mary had spoken to me to turn back and remain bound (if that was an option for me) but I didn't. I chose to fight to remain free in Christ! I always knew that there was something holding me bound. I felt that there was a blockage but I didn't know what it was so now that I knew that I had a generational curse operating in my life, by all means there was no turning back.

That night was just as hard as the night before because the spirits came again. In fact, they were with me that entire afternoon to the point that I was war faring in the grocery store. These bold spirits came up in my face and surrounded me in the store. I immediately got frightened and intimidated. I had no idea what to do so I had to think quickly. I didn't have my Bible with me or anything so I got my phone out and pulled up Ephesians 6:10 and reinforced my armor-the full armor of God.

My oldest daughter Alice was with me and noticed that something was wrong.

"Mommy you ok," she asked. "You look far away."

"I can't talk right now," was my reply. "I am dealing with something right now."

I fought those spirits the entire time I was in that store. For that entire hour I felt that everyone was watching me. However, even though I was uncomfortable, I had to fight off this evil presence. After reinforcing my armor, I played my praise and worship music to get deep into God's presence and prayed in the spirit.

When I got home, I went into the bathroom and waged war against the kingdom of darkness on another level. I went into prayer and I started confessing God's Word and reminding Him of His promises to me. I also reminded the vile spirits of their eviction and reminded them that I had already won the victory through the blood of Jesus Christ on Calvary's tree.

I also reassured Satan that I only serve one master and that is Jesus Christ whom I am sold out to until I die! I was so forceful and loud that my son jokingly asked me if I was fighting demons in there. That night the persistent spirits remained but I felt secure in knowing that I had on the full armor of God. I remained deep in prayer and continued to worship God.

The next day I continued in the fight for my complete freedom as those spirits would not leave me alone. In fact, that awful principality followed me to church, but regardless of my battle, I was secure in knowing that God had me in the palm of His right hand and that He would not put more on me than I could bear.

I had a glorious day in worship at church and the tears just fell as the Holy Spirit fell on me afresh. I was so convicted through my surrender that all I could do was just let the tears fall. It didn't matter who saw me, what they thought, or what I looked like. I was in battle and I knew that I could not win this battle without Christ!

After church, I spoke with Sister Mary and Sister Elizabeth who gave me words of encouragement. I also spoke briefly with my pastor who reminded me that I already won the battle through Christ so all I needed to do was to stand firm in that truth.

Further, he reassured me that once I stay in the Word of God, pray and continue my fellowship that I would get stronger every day until I had complete deliverance. That was indeed the goal. I felt great!

Each day those evil spirits came to check in with me to see if I had compromised in anyway. They particularly loved hovering on the left side of my body. Some days they would get so close to my ear and face that it felt like they were on me. As I got stronger, they came less and less, but there was no way of telling what each day would bring. However, I got deeper in the Word and used my spiritual weapons to fight.

As I stood firm on the promises of God, I got stronger and God spoke to me in ways He had never spoken to me before. He showed me things and spoke to me in dreams. I was dreaming every night and the dreams were profound. Some of them I could interpret and others I needed assistance with.

I also started to have more dreams about myself which I never did. God was showing me things to come and how to protect myself from what Satan was planning. He indeed was refining me and opening doors that He wanted to open in my life.

I didn't even realize how much I was growing until persons started acknowledging the profound words I was speaking. It was at that point that I had to really take a step back and take note. Wow! God is using me in a very serious way to speak into the lives of persons. Of course, I never chose or decided what was said. He would prompt me to speak and tell me what to say. I just complied.

As all of these things were happening in my life, I realized that I still had fear. I was afraid of what I didn't know and what I could not see. I had the generational curse broken off of my life, yet I still felt bound. How could that be? I was getting stronger in Christ as I read His Word, fellowshipped, praised Him and prayed without ceasing.

However, I was doing something that I didn't even realize I was doing. Due to my concern and confusion about what was happening, I contacted my prophetic friend, Ruth. I told her what was going on and she told me the following,

"You are thinking too hard about the spirit world. You need to live your life and focus on your children. You will never be prefect so get it out of your head that you will live a sinless life."

I heard what she said, but I was still confused. I asked her to tell me what God said to her.

"God said to stop worrying," she replied.

Instantly, I felt a calm come over me. I had peace for the first time in a week. All of what I was going through finally made sense to me. What I was doing was allowing my fear to feed doubt and insecurity into my spirit which was allowing an open doorway for Satan to intimidate me. Once God spoke those words to me; I stopped.

At church service the next day, we had victorious proclamations of praises unto God through praise and worship then my pastor spoke a profound word that came straight from heaven just for me.

"There are some people in here who are in fear about something medical or otherwise and they are allowing this fear to cause them to doubt God," he spoke.

I couldn't believe it! God had confirmed His word for me through my pastor. We were reminded that God didn't give us a spirit of fear but of power, love and a sound-mind (2 Timothy 1:7). He immediately told us that if we are feeling that fear that it is not of God but from Satan himself. I felt a shout coming on as I praised God for His faithfulness to me.

After he spoke those words to the flock, he prayed for us then our morning service began. That was the day I knew for sure that I had received my complete deliverance and began to walk in it. That service started our week of prayer so I spent the next seven days in prayer and fasted for God to strengthen me in ministry specifically and our church body as a whole. The scripture focus for this week of prayer was 2 Chronicles 7:14:

"if my people, who are called by my name,
will humble themselves and pray and
seek my face and turn from their wicked ways,
then I will hear from heaven,
and I will forgive their sin and will heal their land."

Once the week of prayer began, I got a call from Sister Elizabeth to be one of the persons to pray during the Thursday night prayer service. She told me to pray about it and get back to her.

As she spoke and gave me the three prayer focus areas, I felt God prompt me to speak on the third one which had the following prayer focus,

> "Rejoice that God is faithful to hear your prayers as
> you seek Him with humility and righteousness."

I felt compelled to speak on this focus area because I knew that this was where I was on my deliverance journey. I had been praying for years. Even when I was in sin, I knew how to call on the name of the Lord and He heard my cry because He knew that I was fighting hard to serve Him.

As I prepared for this night to pray, I spent two days in the presence of the Lord fasting, praying and listening to Him as I readied myself to be used by Him to speak a word to our church family. The Lord surely used me and gave me a profound prayer to release over those present. Those words could have only come from heaven.

I was never a person who liked to pray in public but God used me that night in a mighty way. The prayer was so powerful that I cannot even remember everything that was stated. God had His way in me. However, as I prayed prior to my night to pray, He told me five specific things He is looking for from His children in this season:

1. He wants us to be sold out for Him.
2. He is looking for radical Christians. (The time for passivity is over.)
3. He wants children who will seek Him day and night; night and day.
4. He is looking for humility in His children. (Haughtiness is not of God.)
5. He needs His children to live lives that are holy and acceptable unto Him.

All I knew is that there was less of me and more of Him present. That night a clear message was sent to the kingdom of darkness that the Lord of my life is Jesus, Christ! As I continued to live my life daily for Christ, Satan did try to regain access and his access was denied because all doorways were closed to him. To God be all glory, honor, and praise!

As I conclude this chapter, let me say that I did not feel compelled to get into the details of what The Lord said or showed me, but only to say that in order for God to fully use us, we need to be available. We need to ensure that we have freed ourselves of all strongholds and un-forgiveness in our lives because these are hindrances to us hearing the voice of the Holy Spirit clearly or at all.

God impressed upon me to say that a very important element in this season is having divine connections. I cannot say that this process would have begun for me if it wasn't for my connection to Ruth who possesses the gift of prophecy.

As I reflect, I give thanks for the covering and teaching of my pastor who is a committed sold out servant of the Most High God, because that too is a divine connection. He connected me to Sister Mary and Sister Elizabeth who are prayer warriors and powerful women of God who know how to pray in the spirit and tear down strongholds.

Without these divine connections, I would not be free in Christ nor have complete deliverance today. I pray that this message pricks your heart and starts you on a journey to search your own life for areas of bondage.

People of God, you need to pray to God for divine connections. In this season, if you desire to be successful in your walk with God, you need to be connected to people who are connected to Him. If you aren't then you will have many doorways open for Satan to come in, set up his fortress and take domination over your life.

As you pray and wait for those divine connections, purge your life of people, things, issues, ideals, and habits that are not of God. It will not happen overnight but it is important that you begin the process and see it through to the end (even when Satan turns up the heat on you).

For me, even though I had the foundation of this fortress erected in my life at the tender age of eight, which became occupied by a very strong principality over the years, God was still with me and He still spoke to me and through me. I can't say if that would be the same for everyone because my desire was always to serve and please Him.

Even as I fought to remain free, it was important for me to acknowledge my areas of struggle and pray every night for God to strengthen me so that I could overcome the temptation to sin in those areas. I had to be honest with myself and admit them openly to God so that Satan could not use them against me if I kept them a secret. Hence, I decided that I would keep no secrets from my Heavenly Father.

We beat ourselves up so much when we sin and then we allow Satan to come behind and whip us some more, but God never said that we would not be tempted or that we would not sin. In fact, His word says that God is faithful and would not suffer you to be tempted above what you can handle, but when you are tempted, He will make a way of escape for you (I Corinthians 10:13).

In spite of this truth, I know that when I do sin and confess it to God, that He is faithful and just to forgive me of my sins and cleanse me from all unrighteousness (I John 1:9). I had to remind myself that God does not call us to perfection on our own, but to perfection in Him (Matthew 5:48)! Therefore, my brothers and sisters in Christ, confess your sins to the Lord and find a Christian brother or sister who you can confide in and have them pray for and with you as you seek to become more like our Heavenly Father.

Chapter 31: "Quiet Reflection – God Never Left Me"

I can honestly say that the prayers I prayed to God from the time I was about nine years old paid off because throughout all of my self-doubt, self-sabotage, and low self-esteem, God never left me. He always had this way of letting me know that He had me covered and the most profound ways He did that was through dreams.

As I got older, I can recall God showing me incredible things through dreams and visions; some manifested themselves exactly as I dreamt them, some were warning dreams and others were symbolic and required interpretation.

Even when I made some silly mistakes and made some horrible decisions that could have caused my death, God covered me. Some of you may feel that getting older should have taken the hurt, negative thoughts and anger away or that the memory of the abuse would have remained repressed permanently but it did not.

For me, I continued to struggle with low self-worth which led me into some volatile relationships. At some point along each rugged road, God made a way of escape for me.

There was a time when I was so confused that I started to wonder if I was cursed not knowing that I really was. This led me to the biggest battle of my life which, if I had lost, could have thrusted me into some deep dark places I may not have been able to recover from. It was a long hard fight but through God's grace, mercy, Holy Spirit, Word and my firm stance in Christ, I received complete victory through Christ Jesus.

Even though I am an accomplished woman, Satan cares nothing about that. His job is to abort your purpose by any means necessary so if you don't know who you are in Christ, you will live a defeated life; one filled with one dose of what we call "bad luck" after the other. However, readers please hear me when I say that this is not bad luck. That is some evil force operating in your life that entered through a doorway that was accessed when a door was opened.

You have to now journey to find out what the doorway is in your life, when it was accessed, evict the occupants and deny them further access. You may be able to figure it out on your own but in my case the principality was there for so long (and so strong) that I didn't know it was there wreaking havoc. Hence, I needed heavenly intervention for it to be identified and broken off my life.

Whether you believe what I experienced or not really doesn't matter. Your belief or disbelief doesn't make Satan and his demonic forces unreal. We are living in a world where Satan rules. He is out to kill, steal, and destroy as many lives as possible so we need to be aware of his plan so that we can fight. I am not writing this book to scare anyone. God told me to write this book over fifteen years ago and I was terrified. Maybe He was planting the seed for it to grow for today because I was nowhere near ready to share my life experiences with anyone at that time nor had I yet experienced many of these challenges I wrote about.

However, when He spoke it to me again, I listened and complied. Even though God intended this book to be written for me to help people fight their battles and win, He also used this book for my own healing and deliverance. I now feel like a whole person. I no longer compromise my standards and I decide what or who enters my life.

Today, I am Dr. Samantha V. Evans and I help people accomplish their dreams. I am especially drawn to the students who are rejected or ignored because they are the ones I connect with a lot even though I became a high flyer in school. I am a firm believer that what God allowed me to experience in life was not only for me, but for me to use as a teaching and healing tool to help others who experienced some type of trauma and are now bound.

Even though my teen years were rough and my father and I didn't get along, we have a great relationship today. My father is a great man. I could ask my dad for anything and if he has it; it would be mine. When I told him that I was returning to school to pursue my doctorate degree, he paid my first year in full. That's my daddy!! I love him bunches. My mother and I have had our battles too, but we are doing well. My mom has a big heart. She is a strong woman of God and a rock in many ways. She takes care of everybody. She fed me and my children when we were going through our rough times which I will forever be grateful for. Love my mom!

I thank God for the power of forgiveness that has allowed me to look past all that has happened and love them in spite of it all. I only have two parents so I will love them and do my best to be present and to help them in any way I can. God never promised us that life would be a bed of roses, but He did promise to be there with us through the good times and the bad.

In 2016, I got an opportunity to role-play my feelings towards Grammy Lucy who I feel could have helped me through my pain, but didn't. As I spoke to the fictitious her during the session, I felt so much anger towards her that I didn't even realize was inside me.

The session was very intense with me becoming enraged at times as I asked the question I wanted to put before her for years,

"Why didn't you do anything to help me? All of these years I suffered alone and you said nor did anything."

I expressed such hate towards her for what she did. However, at the end of it all, I told her that I forgave her. You may be wondering why I couldn't speak to her in person. Well, she had Alzheimer's disease and couldn't even remember me. I went to visit her and I had to tell her who I was. I had finally built up the courage to see her after many, many years which gave me peace.

A few months after my visit she died. At her funeral, I felt sadness, but a sense of peace yet again. Why? Well, she was good to us as children and I appreciated that. My only regret was that she did nothing when her husband violated me. However, I am happy that I gave myself permission to forgive her and see her before she died.

Is my battle over? Am I done fighting for Christ? No it isn't and no I am not, but I choose to be happy and decide what and who I allow into my life now. It took me a long time to get here, but I did. I was a victim for a long time and remained one even after I thought I had healed and repented of my sins, but thank God for complete deliverance through Jesus, Christ.

Today, I am stronger, wiser, and armed with the Word of God which makes me a dangerous warrior for Christ and Satan knows this!

My divorce was granted in December 2017 and I received my absolute on January 17, 2018 so the journey to the love of my life continues. However, I find rest in knowing that God has a perfect ending to my story so stay tuned.

Additional Doorways to Sin

In this book I mentioned doorways that I had to fight to deny Satan access through after my deliverance and without a doubt, I can tell you that the fight was plentiful but the effects Satan's access had on my life were worse.

Even though the activities and habits listed on the front cover are ones that you may be familiar with, there are so many others that you may engage in regularly that are doorways to sin. Hence, some of these are through thoughts and actions that you may deem harmless.

Your salvation and deliverance from Satan are so important to God, that I find it necessary to provide you with this information to open your eyes so that you can research them for yourself then decide if they are things you want to continue engaging in.

After reading this information and doing your research, search The Scriptures to find out what God has to say about engaging in these types of acts. Leviticus 19 and Galatians 5 are two good Chapters in the Bible to start with. I further encourage you to talk to God about your involvement in these things and ask Him if they are acceptable to Him. If they are not then ask Him to help you to separate yourself from such people, places, and things (well, that is if your desire is to live for and honor God).

"...through knowledge shall the just be delivered." (Proverbs 11:9b)

These activities and habits listed below are ones that you are possibly familiar with and may even engage in but do not fear, God is the revealer of all hidden things (Daniel 2:22). Hence, this section of my book is intended to help you on your journey to closing doors to Satan so that you can live a fruitful fulfilling life for Jesus Christ.

Marital Arts – Research the form of marital arts that you are involved in to learn about the spiritual influence. Karate in particular involves emptying the mind which can be dangerous. The person is offered a "supernatural" means of defending them self that the average person does not have.

When a person begins to seek this power found in martial arts, they are welcoming spirits of mind control and such to come in and make themselves at home. Such powers only come from God through the Holy Spirit or from Satan through demons (Judges 14-16; Luke 10:19). Karate is also a sport that can invoke the spirit of violence (and in some cases the spirit of murder); all of which a person will need deliverance from (if they desire to live for Jesus Christ).

Yoga – Yoga is a form of exercise that encourages persons to empty their minds as they seek energy healing along with better mental and physical health. Jesus warns us about this in Matthew 12: 43-45.

"When an impure spirit comes out of a person, it goes through dry places seeking rest and does not find it. Then it says, 'I will return to the house I left.' When it arrives, it finds the house unoccupied, swept clean and put in order. Then it goes and takes with it seven other spirits more wicked than itself, and they go in and live there. And the final condition of that person is worse than the first. That is how it will be with this wicked generation."

Rock Music, Fantasy Games, Movies, and Books – these are subtle ways to introduce people to witches and magic (especially children). It is advisable for parents to investigate the activities their children are engaged in during their spare time so that they do not innocently open doorways for demonic spirits to enter their lives. Leviticus 20:6 warns:

"if a person turns to mediums and wizards...I will set my face against that person."

Tattoos – there is much research and articles available on tattoos and how they can attract evil spirits. Leviticus 19: 28 speaks clearly on markings of the skin:

"Ye shall not make any cuttings in your flesh for the dead, nor print any marks upon you: I am the Lord."

God told us not to defile our temple because it is where the Holy Spirit lives (I Corinthians 6: 19).

Idolatry – The Lord made it very clear that you are not to serve any other gods. Throughout the old testament (and some parts of the new), God sets down His laws as it relates to idolatry. God spoke all these words saying in Exodus 20: 1-5:

God spoke all these words, saying:
"I am the Lord your God, who brought you out of the land of Egypt, out of the house of bondage. You shall have no other gods before Me. You shall not make for yourself a carved image—any likeness of anything that is in heaven above, or that is in the earth beneath, or that is in the water under the earth; you shall not bow down to them nor serve them. For I, the Lord your God, am a jealous God, visiting the iniquity of the fathers upon the children to the third and fourth generations of those who hate Me."

Persons who make pledges to Greek gods and other gods to join fraternities and sororities (as well as other such occult groups) have opened themselves up to evil spirits. They need to be denounced if you plan to live your life for Jesus, Christ.

Witchcraft and Warlock Spirits –The Bible says that people who serve other gods belittles God and God will not be mocked (Galatians 6: 7). These spirits offer supernatural power for you to bring harm to another person, get even with someone, obtain riches (fame or power) or to stop a person's progress in life. These types of offerings can be very attractive to someone who feels that God is taking too long to answer their prayers or who has been hurt or rejected by someone.

When a person begins placing curses or seeking to learn about witchcraft, or even seeks to have a witch or warlock place a curse for them, it lets the spirits know that they are welcome in that person's life. God's Word tells us not to seek somebody with occult power, lest we become defiled ourselves Leviticus 19:31:

"Regard not them that have familiar spirits, neither seek after wizards, to be defiled by them: I am the LORD your God."

Deuteronomy 18:10-11:

"Let no one be found among you who sacrifices his son or daughter in the fire, who practices divination or sorcery, interprets omens, engages in

witchcraft, or casts spells, or who is a medium or spiritist or who consults the dead."

Addictions – a person with an addiction is looking for a way to escape some problem of life but in their quest to do so, attracts a bondage spirit which can be hard to break without deliverance. Some common addictions are drugs of all kinds and alcohol. Right here I am referring to persons who cannot live without the drugs to the point where they are constantly high or consume alcohol to the point of drunkenness (Ephesians 5: 18; Galatians 5:21; Isaiah 5:11; Proverbs 201:1).

Fear – The Bible says fear is as witchcraft. That is a powerful comparison because the Bible states that witchcraft is an abomination. In Revelations 21: 8, The Lord says that the fearful will be cast into the sea of fire along with the unbelieving, sorcerers, murders and the like. Why is that you may ask? Well, I am glad you asked. As a result of your fear, those persons who you were supposed to minister too never got to hear the Word of God and died in their sin so their blood is now on your hands. Hence, fear is a spirit that is not of God and He makes that clear throughout the scriptures especially 2 Timothy 1:7.

Self-pity – This type of spirit is very luring. It whispers to the person, "You poor thing! They should not have done that to you!" Once you agree with such thinking, you are welcoming such spirits into your soul (mind, will and emotions). Hence, your pity party can begin! I recall having many pity parties for myself but they didn't make anything better, in fact in the long run they got worse.

We all go through times when we feel badly about something that happened or our current circumstances. Even the great prophet Elijah felt sorry for himself when he fled after Jezebel threatened to take his life (I King 19: 4), but God sent an angel to him to reassure him that God was with him. You must remember that God is still with you during your lowest moments so continue to trust Him and learn to cast your cares upon Him because He cares for you (I Peter 5: 7).

Lust and Perversion – The Bible talks about lasciviousness in Galatians 5: 19. This spirit is a very strong one and once a person starts to think sexual thoughts and act in such ways, they let the spirit realm know that it is acceptable to open the flood gates of such pleasures into their lives. Once this spirit takes up residence in them, this person will begin to engage and think thoughts of lust and perversion. The pull such a spirit can have on a person is very strong and can lead them into some very dangerous sexual territories that can destroy their lives if they are not delivered from such.

Stubbornness – this is doing something repeatedly even after being warned. The Bible calls this being "stiff-necked." Acts 7: 51 says:

"You men who are stiff-necked and uncircumcised in heart and ears are always resisting the Holy Spirit; you are doing just as your fathers did."

The Lord encourages us to listen to His word and abandon arrogance. Such a prideful and arrogant spirit is not of God and the Bible states that such acts cometh before destruction and a fall (Proverbs 16:18).

Tradition – This is a very serious topic. One I can camp out on for a while but I will remain brief. Tradition is a way of doing things that was passed on. It is because of tradition that many people are stagnant today especially believers. God states in Hosea 6:6:

"For I desired mercy, and not sacrifice; and the knowledge of God more than burnt offerings."

Throughout the Bible God gives us instructions on what He wants for us.

However, there are many things that each family, church, or organization passes on to its members that are not scriptural and can become doorways to sin such as tying a black string on a baby's wrist to chase off evil spirits, throwing urine in the yard to protect one's property from evil spirits, and putting spirits of turpentine in the four corners of your house to cleanse it of evil spirits. Beware of these "traditions" that have no scriptural references.

Many people even go to church out of tradition but have no relationship with God our Heavenly Father. Performing this act every Sabbath, serving in the church and doing good works will not earn you a place in the kingdom of heaven my friends. This is a lie from the pits of hell! Colossians 2:8 states:

"Beware lest any man spoil you through philosophy and vain deceit, after the tradition of men, after the rudiments of the world, and not after Christ."

Trauma – this can grip a person so deep in their soul that they can become emotionally, spiritually or mentally paralyzed. Trauma can come in many forms. It can happen due to abuse, witnessing a crime or murder, rape, divorce, losing a loved one, experiencing a near death experience or being in an accident, betrayal, military scars, natural disaster or the like. In Jeremiah 9: 4, the Bible warns us of the cruelty of this world:

"Let everyone beware of his neighbor," [for] *"every neighbor goes about as a slanderer."*

Transference – demonic spirits are transferred through laying on of hands and praying over a person while speaking in tongues. This is not to say that these acts are evil but to say that you must test the spirit (I John 4: 1-3) before you have anyone lay hands on you or speak in tongues over you because every spirit that says that they come in Jesus name is not of God.

Spirits behind cancer – When a person feels like they have been wronged by another, they start to resent that person and sometimes develop a spirit of bitterness and unforgiveness which can affect their health in detrimental ways. However, in their minds they are "getting back at that person" which makes them feel good to be getting revenge. The Bible tells us in *Matthew 6: 15 that when one holds a grudge it will block God's forgiveness for their own sins*!

Further, when a person turns bitter, it invites an evil spirit into their system which will aggravate the cells in their body, which will cause abnormal growths, tumors and such. Unforgiveness has been described by many theologians as poison to the soul and cancer to the body.

Finally, for those persons who refuse to heed God's voice, keep his laws, statutes and commandments, He states in Deuteronomy 28: 27, that He will smite you with emerods (tumors) that cannot be healed. Read it!

Ungodly Soul Ties – this is when you have sexual intercourse with someone to whom you are not married either through fornication or adultery. It causes a person to become defiled and demonic spirits take advantage of such ungodly soul ties. Here is what the scripture says about this in Ezekiel 23:17:

"And the Babylonians came to her into the bed of love, and they defiled her with their whoredom, and she was polluted with them."

Blood guiltiness – this is the guilt associated with one committing a crime or an act where blood was shed. Simultaneously it could refer to any act of grievance, violence, homicide, or even an abortion. Deuteronomy 19:10 (NKJV) states:

"lest innocent blood be shed in the midst of your land which the LORD *your God is giving you as an inheritance, and thus guilt of bloodshed be upon you."*

If you want to determine if an activity or habit is acceptable unto God, you can apply Philippians 4:8:

"...whatsoever things are true, whatsoever things are honest, whatsoever things are just, whatsoever things are pure, whatsoever things are lovely, whatsoever things are of good report; if there be any virtue, and if there be any praise, think on these things."

It is God's desire for us to live happy lives and to enjoy each day abundantly (John 10:10). He never intended for us to live lives of bondage to sin. It is enough to contend with a sinful world but to battle curses levied upon you by ancestors or your own ignorance is just sad. You now have an opportunity to undo the wrong that was done by drawing the bloodline in the sand and say to Satan: NO MORE- THIS MESS STOPS HERE!

It is time to stop allowing Satan to steal your stuff, kill your dreams and destroy your life! How badly do you want to be set free? How badly do you want to live the life Christ died for you to have? God said:

"I set before you life and death, choose life so that both you and your seed [descendants] shall live!" (Deuteronomy 30:19).

It is time for you to be delivered in the mighty name of Jesus Christ!

As you journey towards living a life that is pleasing to God in every way, ensure that whatever you engage in, watch, read or believe does not glorify Satan or portray demonic forces, witchcraft or magic in a positive way because this belief is contrary to the laws and instructions that our Heavenly Father has given us to follow. Therefore, my brothers and sisters, let your life glorify God our Heavenly Father and Him ALONE!

"My people perish [are destroyed] for a lack of knowledge" (Hosea 4:6)

Some of the Information for this section was obtained from Great Bible Study.com, Deliverance Zone.com, Ministering Deliverance.com, Desiringgod.org, and The Holy Bible.

Biography – Dr. Samantha V. Evans

Dr. Samantha V. Evans was born and raised in Nassau, Bahamas. She is a trained counselor by profession and the owner of IT TAKES A VILLAGE Learning, Career and Counseling Center in Nassau. She is a Master Customer Service Trainer and a Global Career Facilitator. Dr. Evans is a college professor with over 12 years of experience as she has taught for the Bahamas Institute of Business and Technology (BIBT) since they were Success Training College. Her desire is to help others develop themselves educationally, spiritually and intellectually, live for Christ and to let His will be done in every area of her life. She is a born-again believer in Jesus Christ of Nazareth and believes that He is the true and living God.

Dr. Evans believes that it is her God-given obligation to share her gifts and talents with those around her so that they too can discover (and live out) their purpose in life. She has a vibrant personality, a humble, helpful, sincere yet stern spirit which makes her appealing to those around her professionally and personally. She is a youth and motivational speaker. She uses both platforms to equip persons with the skills needed for them to make good choices on a daily basis so that they can transition towards their future of greatness. Recently, God has shifted her to focus more on helping people to draw closer to Him, seek deliverance, and learn how to live lives according to His promises for their lives. Hence, she is a firm believer in the power of prayer, worship and fasting. She is the mother of three children: Aisha, Steven, and Peliah.

Please leave a review here on:

https://www.2tigersllc.com/shop/doorways-to-sin-by-dr-samantha-v-evans/

your support and comments are so appreciated!

Stay connected with me or her on **FaceBook**

To book speaking engagements or conferences send email to: doorwaystosin@gmail.com

Or you can write me:

P.O. Box GT-2587
Nassau, Bahamas

Other books by Dr. Samantha V. Evans:

Quiet Reflection Series A, B, C, & D
Books that teach life skills © 2001

Made in the USA
Middletown, DE
26 September 2023